As told by Ordinary Women

Is it possible to use your life to make an extraordinary difference? Yes! *Rocking Ordinary* is a wonderful reminder to moms who want to know that what they do matters. Even when there are piles of laundry and bills and dishes, what you do impacts all your relationships. Lea Ann offers inspiration and wonderful advice on how to walk through the struggles and find yourself in the arms of an amazing God. What you do matters because you matter to Jesus! This is a beautiful book to read and share with a friend.

-Tricia Goyer, *author of 55 books, including* Prayers that Changed History

Rocking Ordinary not only addresses insecurities I feel as "just a regular" woman, but also challenges me to reach out of my comfort zone to others.

Sarah Andrews, *an ordinary wife, adoption advocate, and homeschool mom*

Lea Ann Garfias urges readers to offer their imperfect pasts and presents to God and then allow God to use them to rock their ordinary worlds.

Cindy Puhek, *homeschooling mom of 6, contributing columnist* Home School Enrichment Magazine

Don't let the whimsical cover and title fool you! *Rocking Ordinary* reaches inside you, to those hidden places you don't discuss with other people. Lea Ann says, "Me, too," and walks with you on a journey of grace and hope.

Jenny, *recovering perfectionist, special needs mom, and writer, jennyherman.com*

It doesn't matter who you are or where you came from — if you are a woman that loves Jesus, you need to read this book.

Jackie Card, *homeschooling mom of 4 and writer at oneredeemedmom.com*

Lea Ann Garfias' gifted teaching and storytelling abilities create a roadmap for those who "know their lives count but just want help and encouragement."

Traci Matt, *author of* Don't Waste Your Time Homeschooling: 72 Things I Wish I'd Known

When a woman realizes the truth that the Lord uses her ordinary life to make an extraordinary impact on the world around her, she gets a little braver, stands a little taller, and finds the joy again in her day-to-day calling.

Carrie Lindquist, *blogger at AnEverydayMom.com*

After reading this book, I'm encouraged to rock my ordinary life and be a giver of grace just as Christ Jesus has given me grace.

Pattie Reitz, *wife, mom, reader, writer, teacher, encourager, and friend*

As a big dreamer with a budget, everyday responsibilities, and whose life does not look how she planned it to at this point, *Rocking Ordinary* reminded me that I am a difference maker, and I am needed exactly where I am. My new answer to "How are you doing?" is "I am rocking ordinary!"

Marie Williams, *Writer gal at godpearlsandcoffee.com*

This book takes the ordinary mundane reality of the mountains and valleys and brings it all crashing together. It's like sitting with your best friend over a cup of coffee and having those really good girl talks with some ugly cries that you walk away from knowing you're a better person, better prepared for all that the day brings because you both reveal that you are going through the same thing or you have.

Rebecca Brandt, *homeschool mom and writer at momsmustardseeds.com*

With her whimsical tone and fun anecdotes, Lea Ann masterfully challenges women to change perspective. By viewing our lives as service to God, the focus leaves our tiny selves and turns outward to the enormous world of women just like us.

Betsy Logeman, *ordinary mom*

Coming alongside you like a true friend, Lea Ann Garfias meets you where you are with raw honesty and shows you how an ordinary life is more extraordinary than you think.

Anne Campbell, *homeschool mom of 3 and blogger at mylearningtable.com*

Put down your cape, Supemom, and prepare to find God's love and acceptance and get off the treadmill of perfectionism. Those feelings of overwhelm and burnout end here. Prepare to exhale, laugh, and enjoy *Rocking Ordinary.*

Trisha Mugo, *author at TrishaMugo.com.*

Rocking Ordinary is one of those books that needs to come with a "tissue alert." It should make you laugh, cry, and nod your head in agreement, often all at the same time. Lea Ann speaks from her heart to your heart with a type of encouragement that is too seldom heard. So get out your tissue box, make yourself comfortable, and prepare to be blessed.

Catherine Jaime, *retired homeschool mom of 12, current historian and author*

Lea Ann Garfias reminds readers that ordinary is beautiful and is God-ordained. If you find yourself feeling less than others in your circle or on your social media feed, this book is for you.

Lynley Baker Phillips, *SaveThePhillipsFamily.com*

Rocking Ordinary is a true handbook for Christian women that desire friendship and community on God's level and reminds us that we are in this thing called life together.

Alanna Thompson, *jojoandjennsmom.wordpress.com*

Our ordinary can be super extraordinary if we will let God lead us, and obey Him no matter what season we are in. You will learn to reach out, gain friendships, and lose the fear that has held you back.

Betty Eisenhour, *farm wife, homeschool mom of 7 children, blogging at Peace Creek on the Prairie*

Rocking Ordinary reveals how YOU and I have the power to make the ordinary EXTRAORDINARY every day when we keep our heart set on God and our hands raised in praise and worship!

Audrey Elaine Wall, *wife. mother. friend. Ph.D Candidate at Dallas Baptist University*

Lea Ann's book has in turn made me cry and laugh. Consistently touching my heart and allowing the Holy Spirit to convict me! Thank you Lea Ann for helping me to see and feel "Me too"!

Laurie Banman, *stay at home mamma to one amazing child and helpmeet to my loving husband*

Lea Ann is an absolute breath of fresh air! So many times we as Christians think we have to be perfect and have it all together! Then when it doesn't work, we believe we have failed, which is so far from the truth! This book is so needed in today's "Pinterest"-perfect world.

Laura Prater, *Army wife, and author at RaisingSoldiers4Christ.com*

A quirky read that reminds us all to lift up our souls, reach out to others, and grow love within our families.

Diana Anderson, *wife, momma, & friend, bluebirdsnest.org*

This book is like sitting down with a cup of tea and a friend I didn't even realize I had been deeply missing. There is so much honesty and healing in the chapters of this book.

Debby Gerth, *homeschooling mom of 3*

Lea Ann wants to meet you exactly where you are, in the hustle, in the busy, in the ordinary, messy, busy, non-perfect, kids screaming, everyday life. She encourages you, loves you, and roots for you. She's been there, done that. And knows exactly how to encourage you.

Tina Evans, *wife, mom, and soon-to-be Empowerment Coach for Women*

Lea Ann goes far beyond a simple list of ways to "rock ordinary." Her words, along with the words of Scripture, go deep. They address the heart issues that keep us from following hard after God so that all of the daily ordinary becomes something God can use to shape us and minister His love to others.

Jennifer Janes, *recovering people pleaser and special needs homeschooling mom, jenniferajanes.com*

This book will bring laughter and tears and will help make you spiritually and emotionally stronger. We are NOT alone after all!

Patricia M. Dorsey, *retired school teacher*

This book is for ordinary women everywhere just trying to find their extraordinary. Lea Ann shows us through her wit and with grace how allowing the light of Christ to shine through, we all can be *Rocking Ordinary* everyday!

Kimberly Dewberry, *kimberlydewberry.com*

Lea Ann's words are a comforting balm to remind us that no matter what happens in life we are never truly alone.

Redonna Gochanour, *wife to my BFF Greg, homeschooling mom of our two Amazing boys Big G. and Mr. W., & proud autism awareness advocate*

Reading this book was like sitting down to have coffee with a real girlfriend. She shares her heart, some funny stories, and encourages you in your daily walk not only with God but with those around you and yourself.

Flora Pearce, *stay-at-home mom, full-time student, and amateur hobby farmer*

Reading this book is like talking with a good friend; she's personable, funny and above all else genuine. I'll read this again and again.

Cece Harbor, *mom of 4, writer, special needs advocate, www.rethinkingmystory.com*

Just like sitting down for a chat with a wise friend over a cup of coffee, you will realize you are not alone in your thoughts and emotions as a woman along this journey of life as you read.

Melissa Williamson, *homeschool blogger and pastor's wife, gracefilledhomeschooling.blogspot.com*

Rocking Ordinary is a wonderful encouraging book for all women. In a day where women wear many hats on a daily basis, this book offers grace and builds the bonds of sisterhood. You are not alone, but one of many rocking the ordinary every day!

Jennifer A. Chandler, *wife and homeschooling mama of 4 soon to be 5*

Thank you Lea Ann for writing a book full of godly wisdom, encouragement, and God's truth. Reminding me even though I feel like some days I don't do much, I am in fact *ROCKING ORDINARY.*

Jennie Woelpern, *homeschooling mom and wife of a railroader*

Lea Ann provides an on-time message for women running the race, to be all God has created us to be. What she so graciously reminds us is, the race is not about who crosses the finish line first or if we complete the race in record time, but instead that we NEVER stop pushing toward the finish line, NEVER stop seeking all that He has for us.

Lia Hasier, *homeschool mom*

As we sometimes (well, most times) lose sight as to what it is really all about, Lea Ann exposes it's okay to make mistakes and that we all have struggles and regrets. Most importantly, we have forgiveness, grace, and the unfailing love of God to help us to rise to our highest calling as women.

Deb Zorick, *wife, mother and Registered Nurse*

This book addresses real life ordinary issues moms tackle and offers grace, hope, love, and encouragement through an extraordinary God. If you live an ordinary life but have a spiritual yearning for so much more, this book is for you.

Victoria Richardson, *homeschool mom*

This book has really shed a new light on my ordinary life. I WILL have an extraordinary influence on the future, whether I see it or not. We shape the future!

Elizabeth Smith, *homeschool mom of 7*

Rocking Ordinary has shown me that my story, past, present, and future matter. Nothing is wasted. I matter to God.

Emily Furda, *blogger and rare disease warrior,*
www.JesusInEveryMoment.Wordpress.com

This book is a powerful reminder of the impact we have on those around us. Thank you, Lea Ann for your authenticity and love for Jesus. A must read!

Jennifer Smith, *inspiredbyjennifer.com*

Our ordinary lives don't have to be perfect to be extraordinary. Reading this book has opened my eyes on ways that I can ROCK as a woman, wife, mother, Christian, friend, and leader.

Lindsey Ranger, *wife, stay-at-home mom of three, author of sidebysidelearning.ca*

In *Rocking Ordinary*, Lea Ann Garfias reminds us that even if we think our lives are ordinary we can do extraordinary things. It is a guide, full of advice and encouragement, showing us how to give and accept grace in our homes, relationships, and ministries.

Kerry Jordan, *homeschooling mom, blogger at FishbowlFortune.com*

Have you ever wondered if your ordinary, everyday life even makes a difference? Lea Ann addresses that in this book by reminding us that our Heavenly Father can and will use our day-to-day routines, past hurts, and even our mistakes for His glory, making our lives extraordinary in His eyes.

Jeri Morales, *homeschooling special needs mom of 3*

I laughed and cried with Lea Ann's humorous and gracious writing style. Her transparency to share the realities of motherhood and womanhood in general gave me a whole new perspective of the meanings of failure, success, and even perfectionism. I was left inspired to be a woman who motivates a fellow in need. This is THE uplifting book of the year. A must have in every woman's bookshelf.

Maritza Johanna Antúnez. *full-time homeschooling mom, full-time medical laboratory scientist (ASCP)CM, www.HomeschoolEpiphany.com*

Lea Ann Garfias understands how ordinary lives matter every day and how moms like us keep on *Rocking Ordinary*! This book changed my way of thinking and it will surely change yours as well.

Dana Lambert-Hodge, *rockin' homeschool mom, epilepsy advocate and blogger at Luv'N Lambert Life, luvnlambertlife.com*

The encouragement to ROCK who God created us to be, right where we are, is exactly the message we need to hear today as kingdom women. It took guts to write this book when so many tell us to do more, be more, have more. Get this book for yourself and for a gal pal.

Tiffany Harper, *Beasizeyou.net*

When the introduction to a book moves you to tears and has you lifting up a prayer of thanksgiving to God for using the author to encourage you and to let you know that you are not alone — you know it's going to be an amazing book. That is exactly what you will encounter when you read *Rocking Ordinary* by Lea Ann Garfias.

Amanda Johnson, *a former ordinary stay-at-home homeschooling mother and wife, who is now Rocking Ordinary, faithfamilyfriendslove.wordpress.com*

When the first page grabs your attention and locks you in, you know you have a good read, and this is exactly what happens with Lea Ann Garfias' *Rocking Ordinary*. Lea Ann speaks from a place of passion and understanding, as if speaking to and encouraging a dear friend. Love her sister-girl realness!

Khadijah RBz, *wife, mommy to 3, self-imposed fitness fanatic, and a gut-checking, oily, plant-based foodie who brings light and love to brighten the world*

Rocking Ordinary is a breath of fresh air. Lea Ann Garfias writes with honesty, sincerity and humor. Each chapter left me feeling like my own ordinary life is actually something extraordinary!

Kristin Berry, *co-author of confessionsofanadoptiveparent.com*

Rocking *ordinary*

Holding It Together with Extraordinary Grace

LEA ANN GARFIAS

First printing: July 2016

New Leaf Press, P.O. Box 726, Green Forest, AR 72638
New Leaf Press is a division of the New Leaf Publishing Group, Inc.

ISBN: 978-0-89221-744-1
Library of Congress Number: 2016944052

Cover by Left Coast Design, Portland, Oregon

Printed in the United States of America

Please visit our website for other great titles:
www.newleafpress.net

For information regarding author interviews,
please contact the publicity department at (870) 438-5288.

New Leaf Press
A Division of New Leaf Publishing Group
www.newleafpress.net

Contents

Foreword

You hold in your hand: hope. You may be saddled with motherly stress, too much month left after the money's flown from your purse, or the crushing weight of expectations gone amuck. Even so, there is hope, and Lea Ann Garfias has authentically addressed this seemingly scarce commodity.

Because she's been there. She's walked the tightrope of marriage, parenting, providing, busyness, unrealistic expectations, and relational fallout. What I love about her is her resolve to turn to Jesus in all these circumstances. Not only that, she longs to shepherd you toward wholeness and a realistic view of yourself — you who are wildly loved by God.

Lea Ann and I share the same heartbeat, a similar faith DNA. When I reflect back to the days of my own *Rocking Ordinary*, I actually lived in the exact town she lives in today. I experienced many of the same heartaches and triumphs. And during that time, I wrote a book with echoes of the book you hold in your hands today. *Ordinary Mom, Extraordinary God* was my own testament to the faithfulness of God in the throes of rediscovering biblical womanhood.

Now that my children are nearly grown, I have a different perspective on that busy time of my life. I wish I would've slowed down more, listened more, and reflected more on the moment I stood in. I wish I would've taken more mental snapshots (these in the days before Instagram and Snapchat) of my family just enjoying each other's company. I would've reminded myself that simple family moments slip through your fingers, and you can't ever get them back. So stop there. Revel there. Remain there with joy.

This is why I'm excited you're holding hope in your hands. Because you were made to rock the ordinary, to celebrate this moment, to hold fast to what is true. You are well loved right now, just as you are, right in this place. Whether you meet your high expectations or not does not change the bedrock truth that your Heavenly Father stands in this moment to dote on you, cherishing you as His beloved daughter.

So shed the "supposed to's." Let go of the shoulds. Find freedom as you read. There are no perfect women out there, but a perfectly loving Father awaits you as you are. He will enable you to love your family, forgive the friends who break your heart, re-engage at church, lead with diligence and joy, hear from the Holy Spirit, and manage your life with rest and assurance. There is hope, and it's my prayer that you will dance in that hope as you turn the last page.

— Mary DeMuth
Author of 31 books including *Worth Living: How God's Wild Love Makes You Worthy*

Your life makes an
extraordinary
difference.
You are rocking
ordinary.

Introduction

Let me get something off my chest: I'm not a celebrity. I have never written a *New York Times* bestseller, I don't have my own reality TV show, and I'm not a diet spokesmodel. I have never built a multimillion-dollar business, no one asked me to star in their luxury car commercial, and I don't own a trendy restaurant. I'm just your basic, run-of-the-mill, ordinary mom and wife.

Which is probably what you and I have in common. I'm guessing you don't introduce yourself as a *great woman* or *tremendous influencer* or *leader of many*. Because, quite frankly, most of us don't consider ourselves great. Stuck in an endless routine of cleaning, cooking, and caring for family members, we struggle to find meaning and worth in our daily lives. Exhausted at the end of another busy, chaotic day, we wonder if we have made any measurable progress, if it even matters, if our work even counts.

At least that's how I feel. My friends say they do, too. And I'm pretty sure you, new friend, agree. We don't have fancy titles or thousands of followers. We aren't CEOs or wildly successful entrepreneurs or mayors or beauty queens.

We're ordinary housewives, mothers, friends, church members, and citizens of a community. We drive minivans and shop at Target and wear jeans almost every day. We're feeling pretty insignificant, powerless, tired, undercaffeinated, underappreciated, and even discouraged most of the time.

But that's not the whole truth. We are much more than that.

You and I have probably never met, though I hope someday we do. I hope if you run into me at Starbucks, you grab me to tell me about how you are using your life to make an extraordinary difference — that you are rocking the ordinary.

I Believe in You

Unless you are a friend of mine here in Texas, we probably haven't met yet. If you *are* a local friend and I've already forgotten your name because I have inherited my mother's early-onset slowly-losing-my-mind, reintroduce yourself to me, and I'll be thrilled to know you all over again. But even though we haven't yet shared coffee, *I believe in you*. I believe you are amazing and talented and capable and living a life of tremendous influence.

You are. Do you believe it?

Maybe not yet. And that's ok. It is hard to believe that the omnipotent God, Creator of all the universe, wants to use everyday, ordinary women — your typical suburban housewives and mothers and working-hard-just-to-scarf-down-supper gals who are too tired to stand up straight without two pots of coffee, three chocolate bars, and insole support.

But that is, indeed, who He uses.

I only recently came to understand that. I'm still learning it, actually. Which is why I am writing this book. I need something, someone to explain to me what *really* matters, what the work and the laundry and the frustration and the late nights and the bills are all for, why I should keep caring and dreaming and loving. *I need to know this all matters.*

But I don't find an easy answer. At first, I thought maybe there would be a speaker or an expert or a book or something. Instead, God seemed to tell *me* to write this book. I can't wait until it's done so I can find out how it ends.

It's hard to get to the end some days, though. I feel like we work so hard and the laundry keeps piling up, almost as fast as the dishes in the sink and the appointments on the calendar. How do I get from the busy, crazy now with the crying babies and the minivan problems and the soccer snack schedule and the school papers and the bills (always the bills) to the end where we, along with all of God's love, *win*?

I used to think success was doing some big, giant service for God. As a child I read about those holy women who risked their lives to spread the gospel on the other side of the equator, telling naked murderous tribes of God's love and winning the admiration of every Christian American teen girl along with jewel-encrusted crowns in heaven. That would be me, some day. Until God told me at the age of 20, "Absolutely not." So I failed at missions, apparently.

Then I thought maybe I would win by being Super Christian. So I spent my twenties working hard for grace (yep, you read that right), wearing all the right clothes and listening to all the right music and having all the right friends. I walked to church in the rain in high heels. I led ministries every day of the week. I sat in the front row every Sunday, my children's hair plastered down straight, and smoothed down my skirt under my Bible and sermon notebook and flashed my winning, holy smile. I even reached the epitome of American Holiness — *church staff member.* But God said, "Now, you're done." Done? At 30?

I sure wasn't done trying. I tried Perfect Suzy Homemaker. Perfect Happy Homeschooler. Super Mom, Super Wife, Super Woman. When it came right down to it, I was as good at perfection as I was at squeezing my super rear into a leotard. Not pretty, and only my husband would love it.

My man did love me through each and every attempt to super-awesomize myself, shaking his head and murmuring calming, affirming love over my crazy attempts to make myself matter. Ironically, the most important man in my life taught me the most about how to be a woman.

But meanwhile, a young lady was growing up right there beside me. Overnight, this little girl in pigtails, pink T-shirts, and plastic purses matured into a young woman. I suddenly found myself biting my tongue, checking my grumblings, and watching my words because someone was examining *my* womanhood, and I wasn't sure what kind of pattern I was demonstrating.

How can I give her, my favorite representative of the next generation, the keys to female success? What secrets for greatness can I bestow, when I struggle myself every single day to find the meaning in the madness? The stakes rose suddenly higher, now that it wasn't just my own life but hers, as well.

So I started looking around at you, friends. Some of you seem like you have it so together that I try hard not to mutter unkind things (it's easier to love someone whose kitchen sink is dirtier than yours). But when I started to really pay attention, I noticed a pattern.

Everybody Struggles

Some are straining through marriage. Others are frustrated with children. One with a dying husband. Another with a crummy job. Special needs, difficult in-laws, sickness, divorce, natural disasters, tragedy. We all bear our own burdens; some just reveal more about their problems than others do.

Does this mean we don't matter, that we aren't making a difference, that all we can do is just exist for this season or this year or this life in hopes that we don't make things worse?

Perhaps that's what the enemy wants us to do. It's the biggest lie that Satan uses against us — that we are not like God. He told this to Eve in the garden, whispering to her that she needed to grasp more, do more, become more to be anything like the Creator, to have any kind of power or understanding.

But in reality, she was already created in His image. *She was already like God* in so many, many ways. When she stopped recognizing that, stopped praising Him that she was fearfully and wonderfully made, stopped boldly obeying Him by using her gifts and abilities to their fullest, she lost it. She lost the radiance, the presence, the power of God in her person.

I sin the same way.

Marianne Williamson could have been talking about my innermost thoughts when she penned her famous paragraph.

> Our deepest fear is not that we are inadequate. Our deepest fear is that we are powerful beyond measure. It is our light, not our darkness that most frightens us. We ask ourselves, Who am I to be brilliant, gorgeous, talented, and fabulous? Actually, who are you *not* to be? You are a child of God. Your playing small does not serve the world. There is nothing enlightened about shrinking so that other people will not feel insecure around you. We are all meant to shine, as children do. We were born to make

> manifest the glory of God that is within us. It is not just in some of us; it is in everyone and as we let our own light shine, we unconsciously give others permission to do the same. As we are liberated from our own fear, our presence automatically liberates others.[1]

So how do we recapture that radiance? How do we shine forth the image of God, powerfully reflecting His presence and His purpose in our lives? How does this ordinary, everyday life create extraordinary changes in our homes, our churches, our communities?

This is true success. And that's what I want to achieve for myself, for my daughter, for my neighbor, and for you, friend. I believe that God who called us to glorify Himself will do it through us (1 Thessalonians 5:24). We can, indeed, rock our ordinary lives when we reach out and change our world, one ordinary day at a time.

This book is just the start. You and I and our friends and daughters are going to look hard at what it means to be a real-life woman of influence today. We're going to look at the reality of our lives right now and find meaning, hope, and ministry within our own everyday routines. We're going to study what Scripture commands us to do with the power God has given us. We're going to get out our private journals to scratch out our innermost thoughts and fears and longings. We're going to reach out and form book clubs and Bible studies and prayer groups to wrestle with these truths alongside our friends and even help them make greater impact right where they are. We're going to change the conversations we have with our daughters and their friends, giving them a greater perspective than what they hear on TV and social media and at school.

To get started, go to lagarfias.com/rockingdownloads to get your journal pages, action plans, and more.

We're going to start rocking ordinary. Right now. Join me?

---

1. Marianne Williamson, *A Return to Love,* https://en.wikiquote.org/wiki/Marianne_Williamson, accessed June 25, 2015.

Success and Failure

Part I

God uses our
ordinary lives in
extraordinary ways
if we have the
courage and the
faith to simply obey
wherever we are.

1

Run with Patience

I have a fear of failure. It goes all the way back to childhood. I cannot remember a time I was not afraid of failing.

But fail I do, every day, and always have. Failure seems to be a constant companion, an albatross, really, the decaying reminder that I am all too flawed and corrupted. Everywhere I look, I see evidence of my organization failures, decorating failures, and housekeeping failures. I serve failed recipes. I throw out failed projects. Don't even get me started on fashion fails, diet fails, gardening fails, and scheduling fails.

When I was six and seven, failure's name was *spelling.* Actually, *spelling* is still defined as my failure. To read me is to understand my thin hold on the conventions of English letters. They seem to come and go as they please within my words. I don't understand why everyone else seems to be offended by that.

And my teachers have always been offended by my lackadaisical attitude toward spelling. They got all wrapped up in their shorts and broke out the red pens if my *i* was not always before my *e* or what have you. I got perfect grades in elementary, except for spelling. And maps. My sense of direction is as great as my possibility of winning the National Spelling Bee.

If I thought teachers obsessed over my spelling problem, they could not compare to my parents. It didn't matter if I got all As on my papers in every other subject. Those Fs in spelling sent steam out their ears. They reprimanded me. They punished me. They forced me to copy words dozens of times every day and quizzed me for hours on end. To no avail. I still can't spell.

So after one year of this humiliation by spelling test, I took matters into my own hands and did what any bright young girl in bobby socks and brown oxfords would have done. I hid my spelling papers. One school desk will hold an amazingly large number of spelling tests, no matter what the grade, and it never so much as whispered a word of condemnation. Why air my dirty laundry before the world? No one needed to know my secret shame.

Until my teacher looked in my desk. You can't have any privacy anymore, especially not in a school classroom. She not only invaded the sanctity of my desk stash, but she also removed my property and handed it over to my mother.

I remember the words that came next, the vengeance on my mother's face, the anger amplified by raised voice and stinging paddle. The bruises on my bare backside and legs would eventually heal, but the cutting words etched *failure* deep within my spirit where the scars tightened and hardened with repetition. For years I could neither spell nor repeat what she told me that afternoon, but that was one lesson I would not forget. Do not get an F, do not hide your school papers, do not let the teacher give a bad report.

So at the ripe old age of seven, I learned a valuable lesson — *you cannot hide your failure.* It took me two more decades to learn the more potent reason why — *everyone fails.* Parents fail to prevent their child's failures. Women fail to conceal their fears. The angry fail to hide their temper. The stronger fail to care for the weak. The addicted fail to fix themselves. The hurting fail to heal themselves.

Christians Fail to Live Sinlessly

I grew up in an environment that liked to deny that fundamental truth of humanity, that all are sinners, that we all fall short, that we are all flawed failures. We were good people, in good homes, in good churches, singing good music and reading good books and raising good children in good schools and good neighborhoods. We were so good, you wouldn't believe it.

We shouldn't have believed it.

Because once the real failures come — when the job is lost, the child strays, the marriage ends, the addiction is revealed — no one knows how to handle it. We gasp and look away, unable to help, unable to cope, unable to carry on. Everything is ruined.

If success is perfection, though, no one ever achieves it. We know that truth somehow, way deep inside ourselves; and sometimes the reality of it keeps us up at night or causes us to stare blankly out the kitchen window in despair. Why do we behave, then, as if perfection is a real possibility?

Why do we define our worth, our impact, our success, on the impossible prospect that we can have it all and we can do it all?

I don't know, but I know we do. We think we will be a success if we check off all the good things:

- Perfect, loving, harmonious, romantic marriage to a heartthrob who quotes the Bible and makes good money
- Perfect, respectful, obedient, smart, talented, healthy children who quote the Bible and make good grades
- The right church
- The right job
- The right zip code
- Good clothes
- Good food
- Good friends
- Popularity
- Position
- Fame
- Recognition

We think we can have all that and more if we try harder, live better, and manage our time and our finances.

But it doesn't work. We fail every single day, and then we finally give up on ever being a success. Because in the real world, we look around ourselves and see the laundry hidden under the bed and the baby screaming instead of sleeping and the husband we just had words with and the bills and the leaky roof and the dirty minivan and the garden of weeds and the ill-fitting clothes and say, *Enough! I'll just stuff it all in the back of the closet and live in the closet with it and hope no one knows the truth about me because I'm a big FAILURE.*

That's the lie Satan wants us to believe. When we listen to the lie about *what success is* then we also believe the lie that *we will never be successful.*

It's a lie. The truth is much more powerful and much more intimidating: success grows within our failure, because of our failure, through our failure.

How do we find success, then?

Someone once said, "Success is finding God's will and doing it." God defined success to the young leader Joshua as knowing God's Word and obeying it (see Joshua chapter 1). And though that can encompass so many, many parts of Joshua's life — and mine — I can't help but notice what God *didn't* say was true success:

- His marriage
- His children
- His job
- His wealth
- His health
- His decorating
- His clothing choices
- His diet

You can likely list more things. It feels good, doesn't it? So many things, things we have little control over, do *not* define our success. This list includes many aspects of our lives, even obstacles to overcome, but they don't determine our impact.

Joshua had a clear blueprint from God — follow His plan and be successful. He did, and he was. It seems pretty simplistic for us moms now, but it was not easy for Joshua at the time. Remember, he was saddled with relocating and leading into battle over a million people who had just led Moses to the grave and had tried the patience of the Almighty until even He wanted to wipe them off the face of history.

I wonder if that's why God took the time to talk to Joshua about what success really means. It didn't mean sinless perfection, it meant following God. It meant living and saying His truths no matter the consequences, no matter the obstacles. It meant glorifying Him by courageously living out all God commanded him. It was trusting God to take one life and to make it extraordinary.

We can do that. We can be successful. We can be influential. We can change our world if we do just that — live and say His truths no matter the consequences, no matter the obstacles. We can see God use our ordinary lives in extraordinary ways if we have the courage and the faith to simply obey wherever we are.

So what does success actually look like? That, my friend, is the million-dollar question. That's what all the self-help books in Barnes & Noble are all about — promises of new definitions, new formulas of success.

The problem is that all those books are written by and for 40-year-old men running successful companies or women CEOs who want us to lean in and take charge and make millions. That's not the kind of success you and I are about, though, right?

But since that's the only measurement of leadership or of success we are presented with, it's easy to characterize ourselves as failures. We think our influence is too small, our lives too insignificant. The day-in-day-out drudgery of chores, children, family, and finances takes it all out of us, leaving us with little or no hope for lives of influence.

But we're wrong.

Our View of Success Is Wrong

This morning I'm typing in between rubbing my sore left leg. I pulled a ligament or tendon or something on the back of my ankle a few days ago running my first 5K race.

If you have ever been a slightly overweight mother of four with arthritis and asthma, you would find a way to mention that you had just run your first 5K, too. (Don't judge me, you know it's true.)

I had a great time, though. Other than that entire last mile, when I was sure I would die right there in front of everybody. Other than that, it was a blast.

You see, I live in a really great town in Texas. It has been voted "Best Small Town to Live In" and "Most Boring City in the

Country" and "Playful Town USA" for good reason. It's just a safe, family-friendly suburb in arguably the best state in the union. I am so grateful to live here.

I say that to explain the atypical attitude of the runners here during our Freedom 5K down Main Street. As one should expect in a town with over 35 churches, most of the residents are Christians. So after the first mile, when the sweat ran into my eyes and my shoes grew suddenly several pounds heavier, strangers racing past me would call back encouragement over their shoulder. "They that wait on the Lord will mount up with wings as eagles!" and "You can do all things through Christ!"

My favorite running passage is from Hebrews 12:1–2. The New Testament is full of sports analogies, and Paul the Very Fit Apostle seems to be particularly fond of fighting and triumphant wins. But this passage by the unknown writer of Hebrews was clearly written for us middle-aged, flabby-bellied, plodding mothers who question why they even bother tying on ugly running shoes just to lose.

"Let us run with patience the race set before us," the author writes. He doesn't chide or command or rebuke, just invites me to join him on the marathon. It's a finisher's medal we're after, not first place or even age-category winner. Just complete the race we're on.

With Patience

When I started off my Epic First 5K, I found myself running faster than usual. Carried along by the tide of runners, buoyed by the adrenaline of the moment, I exalted in the pound of my feet on the pavement at the brisk, new pace. It was attainable. I was keeping up with "real runners" and feeling oh, so proud of myself.

That feeling lasted through the first mile and even into the second. But somewhere along the last mile my real self caught up with me, stumbled, and gasped for oxygen. What in the world did I think I was doing? Who did I think I was, anyway, a real athlete? For crying out loud, I couldn't run as a child; what made me think I could do so now?

So there I was on the last mile, the winners and my young son having crossed the finish line five minutes ago. Wouldn't it feel so good to just sit down? Sit, then lie down, then sleep, then forget this ever happened.

But I wanted that finisher's medal so badly. I wanted to wear it, to hang it up on my mirror at home, to take that Instagram selfie at the finish line and declare, "I ran it! I did it!"

Yet God simply asked me to continue going at my own pace, to patiently continue putting one ordinary foot in front of the other patiently.

That's all we wives, mothers, friends, and coworkers are asked to do. God wants us to keep putting one foot in front of the other until we get the finisher's crown.

I was thinking about that during the race when I passed my town's iconic clock tower and rounded the corner to face the finish line. Only one block and I was done; the agony would be past. On both sides of the street, citizens were waving flags and cheering us on, among them racers who had just crossed the line. I squinted through that womanly glow dripping down my brow and saw my husband just beyond the finish line, holding his phone at the ready to snap a picture of my victory. And then I heard, above the crowd, the sweetest voice. "Mommy! Mom, keep going! You are almost there!"

Running toward me up the right side of the street was my 12-year-old son. I didn't know it then, but he had just completed his best running time ever — a full ten minutes faster than his previous best — to win second place in his age group, running the entire time looking back over his shoulder, hoping I would catch up (optimism runs strong in that one).

He broke through the crowd to hand me my inhaler (I told you I was your coolest friend ever) and to jog beside me that last leg. My spirit soared, my steps flew, my fatigue vanished as he brought me the rest of the way over the finish line. If you see a picture of me in that moment, I have this crazy grin on my face. You'd swear something was wrong with me. It was the euphoria of the moment, I think. I knew that I had made it to the end only by God's grace and the help of my family and community.

Seeing we are "surrounded by so great a crowd of witnesses . . . let us run with endurance the race that is set before us" (Hebrews 12:1). Hebrews chapter 11 lists a few of those in our cheerleading crowd — saints and martyrs who have made it across the finish line and are looking for us to follow them. But on race day, I realized that you and I have our own crowd surrounding us regularly. Friends, family, and church members who are passing by, calling back verses of encouragement and smiles of love, reminding us to keep putting one foot in front of the other. I want to be that message of hope for those around me, and I know you do, too.

I want to be like my young son. If I race ahead and make it to a milestone before my friend or neighbor, can I wait around for her, cheer her forward, even come alongside while I'm aching and tired to make sure she crosses the line at her best? I don't want to become so myopic about my own course that I can't see those around me who really just need a word of encouragement or a paper cup of water or a friendly hand of help.

My son remembered that day what I often forget: we aren't competing against each other. We ran in the same race on the same day, starting at the same time and passing the same checkpoints. But he was not competing with me, nor I with him. We each finished at our own pace, doing our own best. He can't compare his time with mine. We have different abilities, different challenges to overcome, different bodies, and different backgrounds. We ran the same course, but it was a completely different event for him than it was for me. He knew that, and that's why he could be just as happy for me with my mediocre time as I was for him with that silver medal around his neck. He was ecstatic I had achieved my goal; I was overjoyed he had won. We shared each other's success so completely.

Different Races

This is why success and failure, winning and losing, running and finishing, look so different for each of us women in our daily lives. *We are all running different races.* We pass each other on the same course, and we call back to one another words of encouragement and verses of hope. We help each other over the rough spots, give a hand up the hills, and pass back cold water or hot coffee to drink. But still we go on, each of us at our own pace, dealing with our own unique difficulties and circumstances.

We have different marriages. Some of us married young; some waited awhile. Some seem to fit together like a glove; others have faced innumerable trials. We overcome different backgrounds, cultures, struggles, health issues, family members, and financial difficulties. Even the seemingly picture-perfect fairy-tale romances like mine have times of despair and turmoil. Marriage is hard.

Some of us are single and at different places of contentment or expectation. I have friends who have always known they would be single, while others truly struggle to know God's will for their marital status. My single friends face their own battles with loneliness, finances, safety, career, church involvement, and significance. Their race looks much different than mine.

Those of us with children are running very different races with each of them. While I was plodding along behind my son in the 5K, a friend of mine was racing with her little boy. She sped past me early in the race, then I passed her up when she slowed for her little guy on the hills. I had the joy of cheering her on and giving her a big high five when she crossed the finish line a couple minutes after me. And then I learned that her older son had just beaten mine in the young runner group.

That made me think about all the mothers I know racing with me in the childrearing marathon. Some of my friends have exceptional children and their Facebook feeds are filled with gold medals, scholarships, and other awards. I can struggle with envy when I see the pictures of my friend's children who consistently win medals weekly. Yet a couple of times a year when I cross paths with Valerie, she reminds me with a smile how tired she is and how worth it the race is to her. Then I walk away encouraged to do my best for my children.

Other moms in my Facebook news feed are at different stages of their race with difficult obstacles to overcome. Some are working hard to adopt, facing issues with the foster system and finances and courts and family members as they take on that herculean ministry of love. I cry when I pray for them.

Others are battling special needs, hanging back in the race to lift their child up and to give him the best support possible so that he can finish at his very best. I have so little concept of what the race looks like for them every single day. I can only pass a cup of water in silence.

We have so many differences in our races. Where we live, whether we work, our finances, our health, our family size, our ministries, our extended community — so many factors make the race completely altered for each one of us.

The truth is, though, that we are all in it, we are all running it at the same time, and we are all commanded to continue moving forward with patience.

We aren't looking at each other, except for encouragement. Never comparison. We are looking to the finish line, to Christ who started it all and will hand out our finisher medal at the end. He ran it ahead of us, and we will enjoy the celebration with Him at the end.

So, my friend, let's tie our sneakers and get back in the race. Just put one foot in front of the other and do your very best. Look ahead, encourage those you pass, and keep going with patience.

What does the Bible say?

Read Joshua 1 and Hebrews 11:1–12:3.

What does it mean to you?

Journal your answers and discuss with a friend.

1. Where do you imagine yourself to be on your race?
2. What is your pace? Are you running or resting?
3. What unique obstacles do you face that make your race different from that of your friends?
4. How can you encourage those you pass or who pass you on the way?
5. What kinds of failure do you fear? How do you overcome that fear?
6. On those weary stretches of the race, how can you continue on in patience?
7. In your own words, what is *success*?

We tear down the walls between us brick by brick every time we reach out and say, "Me, too."

2

Do Not Be Afraid

I led a frustrating choir practice last Sunday. It wasn't anyone's fault, it just felt like everything was against us no matter how hard we tried. A third of the small group showed up late, and the men were unusually chatty. The whole choir sluggishly displayed a clear lack of adequate coffee consumption. I spent most of the practice reiterating and reviewing the exact concepts, parts, and performance techniques we had spent the entire hour rehearsing the week before. It felt like we were getting nowhere.

But I wasn't the most exasperated person in the room. One very, very pregnant alto had her hands full with two toddlers since that morning's nursery workers were also in rehearsal with her. Within a few brief minutes, the sanctuary was littered with board books, train cars, and dribbled milk. And every time I glanced into the harried mother's face, I was transported back a decade to when I was in her maternity clothes.

Too Many Demands

I remembered what it felt like to be in my twenties and struggling — too many responsibilities, not enough resources; the demands of caring for little children and the stress of paying for them; the pressure to keep everything looking good in public when the nature of young children is destruction. I recalled those years sweating through ministry while shushing children and pasting that stale, worn smile on my face, praying inwardly that those around me would understand and give me grace if not a hand.

So it felt like second nature that morning to pick up a fussing 18-month-old girl and hold her on my left hip while conducting with my right hand. I have been here before, seemingly last month. I know so well what it is like to feel pulled in every direction — ministry obligations on top of growing family on top of busy husband on top of thin finances on top of physical fatigue and so much stress. I have the benefit now of the view from a decade later, when all my babies are walking on their own, even preparing to launch lives of their own, and this magical nightmare of sleepless nights and spit-up and car seats is gone forever. I couldn't stop the rehearsal and tell her to hug her children more, but I could make just one hour a little more bearable.

A father in the choir stopped me after church to remark on the ease with which I navigated through the pitfalls of the hour. Apparently I didn't show the frustration I felt (sigh of relief!), perhaps because I was so mindful that I was not the most needy person in the room at that moment. He made a statement, though, that struck me. Thanking me for being an example to the choir members, he remarked, "You know, most of the young people in our choir this morning won't remember that moment when you scooped up the little girl and led us on with a smile. The difficulties of balancing leadership and family are lost on the young; they have to learn from experience. But I am sure that when they are older, each one will look back and wish they had learned how to handle these situations with grace under pressure. And that's when they will remember you."

He was right about those tough lessons. If I didn't scold the children or chide their parent or chastise the choir members or leave in a huff, it was only because I had learned from many, many mistakes. My cheeks still burn when I remember of the times I made the wrong choices: pushing my children to behave at levels inappropriate for their age, demanding others achieve perfection and stay out of my way, blatantly disregarding the reality that we are all struggling to do the best we can each day with difficult situations. If I didn't lose my temper during that rehearsal, it was only because I had at too many other times.

Expectations

This insensitivity is perhaps the biggest obstacle to our influence, no matter what our sphere of leadership may be. As mothers, as ministry leaders, as teachers, as friends, these unrealistic expectations — both for ourselves and for others around us — become a wall blocking our impact on those around us. We assume others expect a level of perfect performance that is completely unrealistic and even inappropriate for the context. We create an agenda for others' lives completely contrary to the work of the Holy Spirit in each of us.

That Sunday morning, it would have been inappropriate to line up the toddlers on a pew with one board book each and expect them to sit quietly and listen to the choir for one hour (though I tell you the truth, a decade ago I did just that). It would have been unloving to expect a mother to stand and sing with a smile while her daughter tripped over her dress and dribbled milk down the front of herself. The opportunity of the moment, the real chance to make a difference, was to love and to help those big and small. No calling is greater than that ministry of grace.

But those pesky expectations get in the way. We can call these unrealistic expectations by so many names — pride, perfectionism, critical spirit, authoritarianism, unforgiveness, and ungraciousness. The more we examine it, the uglier this sin becomes. Yet we all struggle with that messy middle between *what we want others to do* and *what they actually are doing*. That is when we realize it is far too easy to deny those around us the grace we ourselves desperately need.

Every day I find myself building this wall of criticism in front of myself with heavy, painful bricks. Each expectation I build up seems so reasonable to me until I look at the edifice I've erected. "I hate to repeat myself." "Why can't they listen the first time." "She should be more considerate of me." "Why can't he do anything right." "Why doesn't he just do his job." "It's not my responsibility, I'm doing enough." If anyone threw those bricks at me, I'd be bruised and beaten down. But without thinking I pick them up and stack them carefully in front of others every day until the expectation wall is built so high I can't see others over it, and I find myself muttering, *Why doesn't anyone love and appreciate me?* I'm so lonely behind my self-built obstacle wall, frustrated that I'm not making an impact on those that I have barricaded away with my own critical spirit.

They say (whoever *they* are) that children have to be taught to be critical by growing up in a critical environment. I can't judge the validity of that theory, having been raised with exponential criticism. It seems to me, though, that criticism comes naturally to most people; it's an outgrowth of our own prideful sin nature. It takes conscious effort to be graceful, truly loving and forgiving to those around us.

Marketing experts tell us that the idea of *me, too* is a powerful force. Advertisements that communicate this idea of relationship strongly compel us to action because we want to join the group and feel included. We have a longing to be valued and accepted where we are, as we are. We know deep down inside we are lacking and flawed. No matter how prideful we may become, we can't escape the reality of our own fallibility.

Those around us long for the same — our spouse, our children, our in-laws, our friends, our neighbors, and our church members. They are hurting, they are struggling, they are grasping for hope. We can tear down these walls between us brick by brick every time we reach out and say, "Me, too." I'm stumbling, too. I hurt, too. I'm tired, too. I don't have all the answers; I make mistakes. I'm here, too.

And that is why extraordinary leadership leans down to pick up the toddler, wipe up the milk, and lend a hand with a smile. Your friend doesn't need a list of ways she could better manage her time or train her children or perform her duties. She needs someone to hold her baby a moment, wipe his nose, and say, "I remember walking this road. You're doing great." Isn't that what you need?

It's what I crave every day of the week.

Just a couple weeks ago, I turned to my phone while waiting to pick up my daughter from work. My friend Sue was on Facebook messenger, so we struck up a conversation. Sue and I had been friends years ago while our children were young, before I moved a thousand miles away, and now her son was graduating from high school just a few months before my oldest did the same. We commiserated over the emotions of the milestone, the strange process of emptying our nests. This new stage sneaked up on us both, as we discovered while we sent tearful messages back and forth regarding how much it hurt and how this seemed to hit us out of the blue. When my phone battery died, I walked away recharged from those simple words: "Me, too." She felt it with me, she was walking the road with me, she shared those same emotions and regrets and pride and awe. I'm not alone. I'm going to be ok, because she is ok. She is surviving, and so will I.

My friend had a powerful ministry of influence because she chose *me, too* instead of *why don't you* or *you should have.* As long as I have known her, that has been her leadership M.O. — sympathy and a helping hand. This powerful combination is what earned her the nickname Superfriend.

When we actively tear down unrealistic expectations, we exert powerful change on the world around us. I say actively, because expectations naturally creep up like weeds every day, if you can imagine brick walls growing like weeds. It's an unnatural metaphor that I wish were just as unrealistic in real life. But alas, my bricks seem to spring up and stack high without my notice, and I have to tear them down daily.

That seems all well and good when I'm talking about how I view the world around me. I can purposefully seek out and destroy my own unfair preconceptions about *the way things should be* and *the way people should behave around me.* Unfortunately, I have little control over the bias bricks others hurl at me or build up against me. And when I lose *control,* I naturally gain *fear* — a bias of my own that assumes a high wall of dislike or distrust standing between me and my world.

After criticism, this fear of others is the next most powerful force against our influence.

Granted, often times that fear is well-founded. People can be cruel. Our social media age of telling exactly what we think in 144 characters or less has eroded the façade of social graces our grandparents so carefully constructed. We can't go out of the house anymore without wondering if we'll end up on the "before" section of a meme or on a list of worst-dressed — published or private. We see the catty blogs and buzzfeed lists and wonder what people are saying about *us* behind our backs. It's scary.

Sadly, Christian women seem no less critical than the rest. I recall a church greeter who used to inform every woman what was wrong with her makeup when she arrived each Sunday. It was so humiliating, I took to entering by the back door to avoid the scrutiny.

If you really want to feel exposed, be the first woman in your denomination or section of the country to lead a public ministry, and then march across the platform and stand with your back to the entire congregation for a full five minutes once a week to then turn, smile, and teeter down the stairs in high heels. I wanted to die every Sunday morning at 10:13 a.m. when I conducted the church choir in my mid-sized East Coast church. I'm being really honest — I prayed several times that the platform would open up and swallow me alive, Old Testament style. I was so sure the majority was shooting daggers at my rear that live burial would have been a definite improvement. It took me over ten months to overcome my embarrassment, and then shortly afterward, the pastor informed me that a deacon *did* regularly complain about my clothing and appearance. I wish my pastor had kept the secret from me. The only thing worse than imagining people are criticizing you behind your back is finding out they actually are.

But into every life a lot of criticism must fall. It is tempting to crawl into a cave and hide. I've tried that. Not the cave *per se,* but a darkened room with the shades drawn and the phone off the hook. Hiding seems to work for a while, but it is far less satisfying than one would imagine. Not to say there aren't seasons for hiding out; there are. There is a time for rest, recuperation, and recovery. It's important to keep in mind, however, that those are means to an end. The goal is to get back into the game.

My favorite example of this is Elijah in 1 Kings 19. The prophet had been working non-stop — preaching, traveling, miracle-ing. He was beyond spent. And every time Elijah turned around, someone was criticizing him to his face. The queen was out to kill him, literally. Sure, he saw wild success with his open-air revival meeting "Fire from Heaven" on Mount Carmel, but the critics really got into his head. At the end of his rope, Elijah ran away from it all, threw himself down on the desert ground, and begged God to kill him (see, my request that the earth swallow me whole wasn't that unreasonable).

But just as God sustained me, the same way He holds you up each day of your ministry, God tenderly cared for Elijah. First, he met Elijah's physical needs with nourishment and rest. Then he gave Elijah a month to work through the emotions. Finally, the Lord revealed Himself, His Word, and His Will to His waiting servant.

God cares about us. God sees the walls we face, and He knows the bricks hurled against us. Our Heavenly Father recognizes our physical and emotional frailties, and He does not expect us to hurdle every obstacle every day while keeping every hair in place. God cares for us, replenishes us, refuels us, and then sends us right back to the work He designed us to do.

Keep On Keepin' On

And we must boldly keep going. Overcoming our fear of criticism is crucial to leadership. If we would lay aside our fears, we must first know that our work is crucial. Our work in our marriage, our work in our children, our work on our street, in our church, and in our community remains our mandate from God, the reason for which we are created, the means by which we glorify Him. The need around us must loom larger than our fears.

Because when we decide to deliberately impact the world around us, suddenly walls appear on every side — walls of prejudice, criticism, hate, and indifference. The bricks are many, yet strong — hurt, abuse, addiction, oppression, legalism, fear, and pride. I think the last two are the most common and the most potent. Fear and pride motivate people to build walls; the root of all resistance to change (and the criticism and obstacles we face is this resistance) is grounded in fear and pride.

The people we minister to are afraid of change, even if they know they need the change. They yearn for freedom from addiction, but they fear life without the crutch. They seek faithful counselors who will speak wisdom into their lives, but they are afraid to open up. They are fighting abuse, illness, rejection, and financial ruin, but they are terrified of those difficult steps toward recovery.

Homemakers are desperate for relief from the constant stress of the mundane, but they are afraid to reveal their ragged state. Wives are searching for significance and adoration, but they are afraid of rejection. Working mothers are afraid they will fail at everything all at once. Women are afraid their work doesn't matter. They are all afraid someone will find them, see them for who they really are, and then all will be lost.

That is where most of the bricks come from. It is hard to recognize that. It's hard to remember that the snide word, the cutting criticism, the uncalled-for meanness is masking a hurting individual's desperate attempts to protect herself. But usually that's what it is.

I picture this wild animal, a nondescript kind of badger/raccoon/possum/bobcat, if you will (because I'm an animal expert, obviously). The creature has a gash, a gaping wound on its underbelly, and the animal is cornered in the wild between a boulder and a rocky outgrowth. Seeing him suffering, I, nature woman that I am, step toward him with a bowl of water and a roll of bandages, hoping to stop the bleeding and give the poor thing some necessary relief so he can rest and go his own way. I don't want the animal for a pet; I don't have a cage or even the means to support it. I just want to give him the little I have, which is also the little he so desperately needs.

But you can imagine what the wild bob-rac-poss-cat does when I approach him. He immediately backs into the corner, pressing his back against the jagged surface until he scrapes himself, causing another minor wound. And Wild Bob snarls, hisses, and bares his teeth threateningly, snapping at me if I step within reach.

Almost every time I meet an unkind person, this Wild Bob comes to mind. The meaner and more vicious the friend appears, the more convinced I am of the severity of her wounds. Trapped between a rock and a hard place, she lashes out in fear and desperation.

Now, you are about to point out that when I get rabies from the wild, wounded bob-rac-poss-cat, it is me who will be hurt the most. And you are right. There are often times that the only wise thing to do is to leave the water dish and maybe even the bandages on the ground and to back away slowly. There is no honor in offering up oneself to the rabid. Sometimes a professional can be called in, someone with the proper experience and training and even equipment to contain the injured, treat the conditions, and rehabilitate the patient. I cannot cure every hurting creature.

Real-life hurting people cause very real pain. This analogy simply highlights for me the necessity of knowing when to walk away. I haven't always done that soon enough; I tend to stay longer than I should, creep too closely, reach too far, and allow myself to be scratched up, bitten, and almost mauled because I'm sure I can effect lasting change.

But that strategy has never worked for me yet.

Instead, by the time I realize that I have no power to do any further good, I'm so badly injured that I have need of help and support myself before I can go on in my ministry. That isn't wise. I need to recognize this sooner.

Christ met hurting people in His own earthly ministry. In fact, everywhere He went, men and women were confronted with their need of Him, yet they seldom reached out for help. Frequently they criticized Him, reviled Him, even chased Him from the town. In Mark chapter 6, we hear Jesus' hometown bad-mouthing His family, His occupation, and His ministry. He couldn't do anything right, as far as they were concerned.

Unlike my first instinct to rush forward with the first aid kit, Christ didn't say, "I'll show them" and proceed to spend the rest of His days proving them wrong. Jesus never forced His preaching on them because they obviously needed it the most. Instead, He healed a few (akin to leaving a dish of water nearby) and then left. Forever.

Jesus instructed His disciples, "Whosoever will not receive you nor hear you, when you depart from there, shake off the dust under your feet as a testimony against them" (Mark 6:11). You're done here. Move on.

There is a difference, then, between running away in fear and simply moving on. The distinction seems difficult when we are in the midst of the pain, but people further removed from the situation — objective observers like our spouse, pastor, mentor, friend — can help us see reality. The difference is found in two areas: our motivation and the other person's openness to change.

We all come to painful times in ministry, relationships, or roles, and wonder if it is time to leave or time to dig in harder. The first question we need to ask is *why do I want to leave?* Is it because I have completed the task God gave me to do here? Is it because I am experiencing more hurt than results? Is it because I'm afraid of what will come next? Why do I want to walk away? There isn't an invalid reason; everyone wants to walk away for various reasons.

Remember even Christ wanted to retreat from His road to the Cross. Elijah wanted to retire from propheting. Moses decided he had more headaches from leadership than he could shake a stick at. It is natural in times of fatigue, stress, and pain to look for a way out. We need to recognize these feelings and to find the root cause.

So honestly tell yourself and your trusted advisor why you want to walk away from the painful relationship or the heavy ministry. Talk it out, journal it, pray over the issues. Peel back the layers of your emotions, which are likely conflicted and complex.

After honestly facing your emotions, you can then examine the second part — the other people involved. Do the wounded *want* help? Are they seeking healing? Are they trying to grow, and are they looking to you for guidance? Or are they malevolent, hurtful, and hateful? The answers to these questions are an indication of the potential for change.

This is a very hard decision. It is easy to become so attached to a relationship, to become so invested in our vision for someone else's success that the reality becomes clouded. When we look at the painful situation, we may only see what we want for them, not where they really are.

This can be especially dangerous when working with those who are severely wounded. Individuals, families, and ministries harmed by abuse, addiction, and violence have deep wounds that need professional care, someone with the experience and resources to administer the tough love and painful procedures necessary for recovery. These hurting people can be so harmful to anyone trying to help that ministering to them remains dangerous and difficult.

Our heart goes out to our friends and family members in these painful situations. We sincerely desire to be the agent of change in their lives. We want to see them heal, flourish, and even grow. But we cannot heal them in our own power. The wounded must first desire to be healed. That's why Christ frequently *asked* those He ministered to *what do you want* before He healed them. They first had to admit their need.

Throughout the healing process, we continue to look for this sincere desire for change. All healing is a two-steps-forward-one-step-back process, but we should find a general improvement over time. What we don't want is a repeated cycle of returning back to old ways, old habits, old sin. That's a clear warning sign you both aren't working toward the same goals.

Moving On?

So when evaluating whether we should go or stay, whether we are making a difference or moving on, we must pray about both our motivations and the desire for change.

We can't oversimplify this, of course. There are usually other considerations in painful relationships and ministries. That's why I find that having an objective counselor is invaluable when working through these issues. Elijah, for example, was so sure his time was up. Everyone wanted to kill him, he thought, and he was beyond exhausted from all the running and preaching and hiding and miracle-working and running some more. God showed Elijah what he had been overlooking — that there were many others still depending on his ministry. Elijah spent time alone beside that brook, away from the crowds, just resting and eating and talking to God, and then he was right back to working with people again.

So our obstacles are not always an indication that we should be moving on. Like Elijah, we must first take care of our physical and emotional selves and spend some time in prayer and reflection before we can clearly see how God is leading. God may be telling us to move on, or He could be showing us where we need to grow. Not every fear is a sign to quit. Most of the time, our exposure to criticism is a chance for personal growth. God uses the trying people in our lives to teach us valuable lessons, too.

A long time ago, a young man in my church was competing in a national trumpet competition, and he asked me to accompany him on the piano. I was happy to do it, because he was a talented musician who was fun to perform with, and the music itself was a welcome challenge. But he was a busy teenager in a large family, and I was a busy working mom with young children, so we struggled to find opportunities to rehearse together.

Criticism

One evening his mother asked if I would come to his house to practice with him. I packed up my three little ones and hauled them in the van to the next town where they lived. When we arrived, my two preschoolers ran off to play with the other children in the house, and I left the baby in his car seat to sit beside the piano where I played.

The older mom walked in, saw the baby sitting there quietly, and asked if I needed her to take him. I told her she was welcome to hold him if she wanted, but that he was fine sitting there listening. "He usually sits in his seat while I teach lessons every day," I explained.

"You leave him in his car seat while you teach lessons every day?" Her eyebrows raised. She repeated the sentence two more times to me, then walked away shaking her head.

My face burned with embarrassment and annoyance. I was going out of my way to help *her son*, and she was criticizing what I did with mine? If I was happy and my baby was happy, why did she need to butt in?

It was a small remark, really, but it bothered me. It festered in my brain. For days I heard her voice echo back every single time I placed the baby in his car seat. I found myself wrestling with my feelings toward the woman; I didn't want to be bitter toward her, but those words (and eyebrows) kept coming back.

Finally, a few weeks later, I asked myself *why does this bother me so much?* If I'm as happy with my decisions as I keep telling myself, what about her remark hit a nerve? When I was honest with myself, I realized that I did fear that I pushed my children around my own schedule. There were changes I knew I should make in how I cared for my babies while ministering to others. I wasn't as balanced as I pretended to be.

Criticism hurts. Sometimes that pain is a pressure point that needs adjustment. So many times when I find myself overreacting to a comment or perceived negativity from someone else, I'm really defending a flaw I know I should correct. That's the worst kind of criticism — the one I secretly feel I deserve.

That's what *constructive criticism* means. I have a chance to grow through it, to admit my mistakes and to become better. I owe that mother a debt of gratitude for the reminder that my babies grow too fast to waste their infancy hurrying them through other people's agendas. Babies should be held more than buckled. I needed to change.

Criticism offers not only an insight into what our needs are, but also at what the critic is struggling with. I look back on the car seat incident differently a decade later. That mother was then where I am now — watching her oldest leave the house, looking back at growing children and empty cribs. She likely longed for the chance to hold those babies again, to squeeze their meaty thighs and laugh at their cute lisps and silly foibles. There I was with what she no longer had: a chance to nuzzle and rock and hold babies for just a few more brief moments.

You likely can think back on some painful, unfounded criticism that left you bewildered until later when you learned *the rest of the story.* The man who constantly pointed out other women's hemlines in the church choir until he was later found to be addicted to pornography. The woman who was always railing about people gossiping about her, though no one knew until later she was hiding an addiction.

Often times, our worst critics are the ones who most need our forgiveness and grace. Ironically, if they are close enough to hurt us, they are standing close enough to be impacted by us. We don't always see what they need or why they are defensive, but in time we will make a difference with them by our gracious reaction and consistency.

When we are criticized, we have tremendous opportunity to overcome resistance. Each time we react with sympathy for others rather than defensiveness, we tear down another brick in the wall between us. Over time, by carefully demonstrating love this way, we do make real change in those lives around us.

How do we reach out effectively during times of criticism? I think there are several steps that help us use criticism as a force for good in our own lives while breaking down barriers with those around us.

First of all, we do well to remember that the critic is not the enemy. The one who is hurting us with accusations and gossip behind our backs or with biting criticsm to our faces is the very one we want to reach with God's love and healing. At all cost — and the cost is usually hours on our knees before God — we want to avoid the *us against them* mentality. We are with them as long as we both want God's best for our lives. This is love.

Secondly, we do ourselves a great service if we can stay quiet. It is so tempting to defend ourselves or to put critics back in their place with that witty and cutting remark. But no one feels good about that the next day. My favorite verse in this situation is Exodus 14:14: "The LORD will fight for you, and you shall hold your peace." Biting my tongue and keeping quiet is not easy. I'll find myself fighting my own mouth until I can get into a private place and let it all out to God and to my husband. Staying quiet in the moment, though, is a great place to start toward healing.

Next, it is a good idea to sort out the emotions in private. I like to journal about it, mutter under my breath, and then pray over it. It often takes awhile before I can just get past my emotional reaction so I can think more clearly about the situation.

I find someone trusted to talk it out. That's usually my husband and my best friend. They both know who I am, flaws and all, and still love me. They are both very patient listeners and know when I am venting and when I am ready to listen to reason. And they are both very discreet. It is important to have a safe place to confide. To heal from the emotional wound of criticism, we need to feel heard by God and a friend.

When the emotions have died and we feel heard, we can reflect on the criticism itself. What does it mean? Is there anything I can learn about myself, something I really should change? Is there anything to learn about the critic, something he or she needs from me? How can I improve my ministry and grow as a result of this experience?

It takes me awhile to get through the stage of examination after criticism. It is hard to overcome my own defensiveness, to peel back my pride and uncover the truth of my sin and need. It's humiliating.

That's why ultimately, when we allow criticism to be a force for good in our lives, we allow ourselves to grow. True, lasting, godly change is only a result of God's work, not of our own human striving. It is about Christ living through me, not my doing God's work my way. These lessons in humility are a necessary part of God's pruning in my life, my relationships, my work, and my service. The more of my sinful self that God removes, the more of Himself can shine through to others.

What does the Bible say?

Read 1 Kings 18–19 and Acts 14.

What does it mean to you?

Journal your answers and discuss with a friend.

1. What frustrating situations have you faced this week? Do any of them represent unrealistic expectations you have put on yourself or on those around you?
2. Next time you face a similar frustration, how can you give those around you the gift of grace (hint — what grace do *you* need?).
3. What trial, temptation, or life experience are you facing that allows you to reach out to someone and say, "Me, too?"
4. In what ways does fear of criticism hamper your effectiveness?
5. What criticism have you faced recently? How can you apply the steps toward recovery to grow through the experience?
6. Are you burdened about a wounded friend or family member who is lashing out? As you pray through this chapter, do you feel compelled to reach toward them or to move on?
7. Do you have wise counselors in your life? Who do you trust to help you in your journey, and who is speaking compassionate truth into your life?
8. Are you that kind of safe friend who offers help and hope? How can you be that minister to someone this week?

Extraordinary friends make the ordinary choice to reach out continually and consistently.

3

Reach Out

There are two things required to write. One of them is a window to look out. The other is food. I don't know why, but I can't write a complete sentence without gazing into the middle distance and chewing.

Every day at 1 p.m., I shoo the children away to their bedrooms with their books and homework and Legos so that I can sit at my desk to write in peace. I have followed the same routine for years and years, only the writing assignments have changed and the children have grown larger. Each afternoon, I sit and stare out the window, watching the neighbors come and go, nibbling on candy or nuts or berries, and pecking at my keyboard, hoping amazing thoughts will magically materialize on the screen in front of me.

Gazing into the middle distance and chewing thoughtfully for an hour or two will work up a powerful thirst. This is why I try to remember to put a big quart-sized water bottle on the corner of my desk. It must be on the right side of my keyboard, just above my mouse, or I won't even notice it's there, let alone reach for it. Two hours, maybe three will go by, and I suddenly feel parched as though from months wandering the desert. I could have a water bottle inches from my left hand yet never take advantage of its refreshment because I am so accustomed to looking and reaching only to the right.

And thus I find that, after a couple of hours of mentally wandering the middle distance out my window munching carrot sticks or banana chips, I am simply parched with thirst. Writing is such a tough life.

It's just like when we spend a frantic day running errands with a minivan full of squirmy children and forget to bring our own water bottle. We may have juice boxes and baggies of Cheerios for everyone, but nothing for the mom. Hence we find ourselves in the grocery store, surrounded by aisle after aisle of diet soda and bottled teas and expensive refrigerated smoothies, but we deny ourselves the 99 cent water bottle because "I can wait until I get home — after just one more quick errand." Then we wonder why our head pounds from the pressure of our needless self-denial, our nerves dry and splintered as a twig in drought, snapping harshly at the slightest whine from our little ones. We are killing ourselves with thirst.

And that, my dear, is how I treat friendships.

I have gone not just months, but years and years of my life killing myself with thirst for friendship. I'm so busy running through my schedule that I don't have time for another relationship just now. I'm so focused on accomplishing the tasks of the ministry that I dash through church services and special meetings, ignoring the relationships and resources available for me on either side of the aisle.

Like every proper homeschool mom, I exert enormous amounts of time socializing my children. The extra classes, music rehearsals, soccer practices, part-time jobs, parties, play dates, and church activities crowd the calendar into a cacophony of social commitments — for everyone but me. It's the dirty secret of homeschooling: everyone gets socialized but the mom.

I thirst for friends every bit as much, nay, more than my children do. I yearn for a kindred spirit, a companion in arms, a gal-pal. My husband is great — no, he's smokin' hot and crazy funny — but he doesn't get coffee, clothes, and mental exhaustion jokes like a true girlfriend. The need is real.

But when I finally realize my thirst, it's too late. I'm already emotionally dehydrated, parched from lack of fellowship. I have companions, prayer warriors, and soul sisters right there at my left hand, waiting for me to reach out, and I don't even see them. All I can see is my to-do list in my right hand. My own life, my own agenda, my own needs grow great in my own sight until everyone else has faded to invisibility.

So I minimize the problem. Seriously, when was the last time we saw a mother keel over from thirst inside the Sack N Save? "Mom down with dehydration on aisle 7!" blares the loudspeaker. Tsk, tsk. Should have brought her water bottle, or bought a coffee on the way in, or at least sipped some of her toddler's apple juice, we think as we nudge our cart around the corpse. Amateur.

Of course getting thirsty isn't that big a deal — until you are admitted into the hospital for kidney problems (don't ask me how I know). Similarly, neglecting friendships isn't that big a deal — until our very souls are on life support.

Needing Others

Those dark days come when we desperately need a prayer warrior, a confidante, a warm hand. The days when the laundry won't end, the phone won't stop ringing, and the toddlers won't stop destroying. The days when the sky falls, the diagnosis comes back, the job ends, the parent dies, the teen rebels, the church splits. The days when all our carefully laid plans and gingerly balanced spinning plates come crashing down, shattering at our feet. The days the dreams die.

Who do we call when we have no words to say? Who do we turn to when the burden sickens our bellies? Who can hold our sighs and our secrets until the skies clear?

God Himself knows we need others, and He declared it not good, not right at all that we be alone (Genesis 2:18). We are created for communion, for companionship. Our togetherness itself glorifies God as His ultimate plan for unified praise.

We need friends, and a friend needs us. It's a basic life principle that we too easily forget, too casually set aside, until suddenly we find ourselves unprepared for troubles.

> Two are better than one,
> Because they have a good reward for their labor.
> For if they fall, one will lift up his companion.
> But woe to him who is alone when he falls,
> For he has no one to help him up.

> Again, if two lie down together, they will keep warm;
> But how can one be warm alone?
> Though one may be overpowered by another, two can withstand him.
> And a threefold cord is not quickly broken (Ecclesiastes 4:9–12).

We struggle to make friends, making excuses instead. I'm shy. I'm an introvert. I am busy at home with my children all day. I work full time. I work from home. My church is too big; my church is too small. The church people are not friendly; there are too many cliques. But that's all we make — excuses. More small reasons to ignore the greatest working of God through me.

> And now abide faith, hope, love, these three; but the greatest of these is love (1 Corinthians 13:13).

God works His love into my life, through my life, out of my life. He reaches out of Himself to love me, shape me, grace me with His likeness, and I reflect Him by doing the same, reaching outside my four walls toward others. God's love sees through my eyes the needs, reaches through my hands toward the needy.

Thus, the shining badge of faith becomes loving friendship. "A new commandment I give to you, that you love one another; as I have loved you, that you also love one another. By this all will know that you are My disciples, if you have love for one another" (John 13:34–35).

So there are two reasons we find ourselves lonely; yea, three situations that find us without a companion: a cross-country move, a selfish attitude, a schedule that leaves no room for others. The good news is, we can cure all of these.

I've moved eight times in my life and across the country twice as an adult. I can assure you beyond a shadow of a doubt that even introverts can make friends quickly in a new town with this simple speech:

> Hi, my name is ______________. I just moved here from ____________.

That's it. Most of the time, a stranger will do the rest of the talking for you after that, maybe asking a few questions to get to know you. They will pretty much fill you in on what you need to know about the street, organization, or store you find yourself in at the time. After that, just accept her invitation to meet at the park / come over for dinner / visit her church. Keep repeating the speech until you have met so many people you can't remember their names.

The second cause of loneliness, a selfish attitude, is harder to overcome, because we first have to recognize it. Indeed, it took me way too long, too many years, to recognize the real fallacy of my thinking. I was focused on the wrong things — friends for *me*. How selfish is that? But of course, I don't *need* friends. As long as I continue evaluating relationships based on *what they are doing for me,* then I'm not going to value the people and opportunities that God has blessed me with. I'm not loving the way Christ loves if I'm only loving myself.

Sometimes I'm not looking to the friend at the left because I'm whining that there is nothing at the tip of my right hand. I demand my friend dress a certain way, educate her children like I do, attend my church, agree with me on politics, doctrine, music, and movies. Stay right in this place, and then I will allow you to meet my needs.

How foolish is that? Such critical attitudes oppose the very love Christ demonstrates on our behalf. The Pharisaical pride in status and association slips into our hearts and lives easier than we care to admit. God places people, loves people in various backgrounds and perspectives all around me. He's calling me to look around and reach out.

Finally, we may be lonely because scheduling conflicts render our calendars more important than Christ-like love. Task-oriented overachievers like me fail to remember that *the things we do are less important than the people we touch.* If I complete all the to-do lists of men and of angels and have no time to talk with a live person, I am a worthless machine or a faithless robot (to paraphrase 1 Corinthians 13).

I was musing over this last year when I ran across an article about the importance of making time for friends. The writer eloquently described my own friendship fears and failures, then told of her bold, new plan: an experiment in which she challenged herself to enjoy lunch with a friend each week for a year. The discipline of making regular time for other women both forced her to reach outside her usual circle and also helped her appreciate the women around her.[1]

The concept resonated with me so strongly that I decided to do the same. But first, I had to make some friends.

You may or may not be laughing, depending on how recently you have counted how many IRL friends you have (in real life, not just social media). Scary, isn't it? We have become a generation of women with hundreds of friends on Facebook but fewer than a handful in our community. We are super-connected across the country and around the world, yet the ties that bind us to our own town and church are thin.

We are a race of very popular hermits.

So what if all the women around me are just as lonely as I am? What if the lady who sits behind me in church or who lives across the street or who brings the soccer snacks is just as desperate for friendship, just as intimidated by rejection, just as unsure how to make the first move?

What if I am the one who is supposed to make the first move? The thought makes me clutch my introverted heart and break out in a sweat.

I'm so incredibly thankful for my friends who made the first move toward me. One of them is still my best friend after taking the first step decades ago. I think we all learn how to be friends from brave women like that, the ones who take a deep breath and reach out to make a difference.

I have learned what others-focused friendship means from brave women — women who left cards and books in my church pew; women who dropped off flowers and cookies on my front porch; women who texted prayers, emailed jokes, and squeezed silent hugs; women who met needs, asking nothing.

But those times I've most needed a friend were the times it was probably hardest to befriend me. The dismal days of depression, the

---

1. Jennifer Dukes Lee, "If You're Feeling Lonely? This Post Is for You," http://jenniferdukeslee.com/if-youre-feeling-lonely-this-post-is-for-you/, accessed March 2, 2015.

long journeys through the valley of death, the trials of debilitating pain. In those desperate moments and months when my soul was parched and dehydrated, I could not even respond to gentle gifts of graceful friendship. But they came, and they still come.

Extraordinary friends make the ordinary choice to reach out continually and consistently. They are friends when there isn't yet a deep relationship. They give when nothing is coming back to them. They expose themselves to intimacy and understanding, bravely risking their hearts for the good of others around them. They sacrifice.

I want to be that extraordinary friend. I know you do, too. We want to reach out to impact our world. Deep within our souls, we know that is why the urge for relationships burns our souls, why since Eve we have never wanted to be completely alone, why we seek help and wholeness from connection to one another.

This loving, life-affirming friendship starts, like all intimate relationships, with the first look. We need to be brave enough, disciplined enough, intentional enough to put down the smart phone, look each other in the eye, and smile. We are all starved for real face time, and we won't get enough until we give each other the eye.

We've become so isolated in our lifestyles, haven't we? Without trying too hard, we could live entire days or even weeks without touching anyone outside our immediate family, without having a face-to-face conversation with even a casual acquaintance. We drive in our nearly soundproof minivans to soccer practice where we sit on the edge of the field just five feet and a light year away from the woman across town, scrolling through our smart phone during halftime. We attend several church services each week, politely smile and shake hands, and never know the needs of the woman across the aisle.

Reaching Out

So we need to practice eye contact and hand contact and even voice contact — picking up a conversation and actually waiting to hear *how you are really doing* and caring if the answer isn't *fine*. A new command for a new habit, a new practice for a new relationship.

So who am I looking at? If I get my eyes off myself and stop looking for my own reflection in everyone I meet, I may be surprised to find my warmest, truest friends in unlikely, unlike-me people. As schoolgirls learn well the lie that *my friends look like me, are my age, and live in my neighborhood,* we seek after another in our own image, crying piteously when no replica is found. But mature love changes us, giving us the power of unity — our differences being one glorious reflection of His ultimate glory (Galatians 3:26–4:3). Our communion with one another becomes a holy social sacrament, a working out of all the grace and sacrifice of Christ on our behalf, shed abroad in words and works of kindness toward one another.

But I mar the reflection of Jesus, shattering the mirror of grace with my scared silence. Introvert, shy, reserved, I label myself unfit for taking the first step in a new relationship. I may come alive on stage with a violin bow or choral baton in my hand, but I will die a thousand deaths before introducing myself to a stranger or telling a casual acquaintance how my day truly feels. Opening up to people is scary, and I've had my fair share of hurts.

So I've memorized *what to do when meeting a stranger.* I can tell you my name and ask yours, shake hands and make small talk, even find a polite way to end the conversation so I can escape out of the room to breathe again. But that's just barely past the first phase of the relationship, and now I hesitate to take it to the next level. It's safer to stay at the "smile and wave" stage. I'm not ready to ask you out on the date yet, unsure how to further our friendship. Instead, I'll tend to hang back and wait to see if you will ask *me* out, and if you are shy, too, we'll both be waiting a long, long time. It was nice knowing you.

This waiting game might have dragged on particularly long because I was under the mistaken impression that the friend-date necessitated a personal invitation to my house. And that is super-scary. I have experienced some really bad entertaining experiences, and now inviting people over has become one of my biggest fears. I'd rather try on bathing suits. And model them. In church. Because that's what having a new friend over to my house feels like — barely covering my innermost intimacies, showing off all my flab and mis-shapen parts, putting my imperfections on display, and exposing my true self to ridicule.

But then I realized something life changing: I could be a friend *outside the house.* I began tentatively inviting acquaintances to coffee, to lunch, to group dinners at local restaurants. And even though I felt like this strategy was still a big risk, no one turned me down or stood me up! Within a month, I had to carefully watch my scheduling because I had at least one friend-date every week. I was socialized.

These friend-dates surprised me. There was iron-sharpening happening right there at the lunch table, every time. Over burrito bowls and guacamole, the Holy Spirit showed up to both encourage and challenge. After those first few minutes of hesitant small talk, some serious sharing started — the kind where we lean closer, make clear eye contact, clutch the coffee mug and our hearts to whisper the scary truths.

The relationship didn't end when we left the restaurant. We began texting each other regularly, asking for prayer and for prayer requests. We shared verses and encouragement, jokes and news, achievements and trials. We became true friends.

My first few months of the friend experiment taught me a powerful lesson: I need to reach out to my friends because we need each other.

I think we always knew that, but we're held back by fear. We are afraid of rejection, we are afraid of criticism, we are afraid of failure, we are afraid of misunderstanding. And it's true, that all will happen. It's a given: we will, at times, be rejected, criticized, and misunderstood. We will fail our friends, and they will fail us. But that's not a reason we should hold back.

That's *why* we need to reach out.

When I hold back, I already fail. In rejecting a relationship, I'm rejecting a real person who needs me to reach out to her in love. I'm inviting and even validating the criticism by refusing to live openly in the truth. I give those around me no alternative but misunderstanding and hurt. I've become the problem, not the solution.

But when I reach out in faith (because it's so scary that it does take real faith), I already win. Building relationships, boldly living my faith, and lovingly speaking truth are extraordinary solutions to an ordinary problem. It's a significant change in my life that ripples throughout those around me. It's the fruit of the Spirit in our Christian union.

When Things Go Awry

Yet sometimes friendship hurts. It's a sad truth. I've been rejected, misunderstood, and publicly and privately criticized. And I have failed some of my friends. There are some friendships that I said "goodbye" to with relief, grateful that the drama was over. But there are some lost relationships that I mourn regularly. I miss them. I wish I could reach out and heal the brokenness between us. But this is not the right time for that.

We simply can't have perfect relationships in this fallen world. Ever since Adam and Eve blamed each other, ever since Cain killed Abel, ever since Ham gossiped about his father Noah, reaching out to others has been hard. Because our hearts are hard. Sin, pride, jealousy, fear, and bitterness harden us from the inside out. Those callouses and scars inhibit others reaching out to us. So it becomes harder for us to reach out to them.

Even so, every time we do reach out of ourselves and toward others, we overcome evil with good. We take the extraordinary step of moving beyond the harshness of the Curse to bless others. We follow Christ's great sacrifice of love with small demonstrations of our own toward our sisters.

That's why we can't give in to petty misunderstandings. We can't let hard feelings or supposed motives or imagined slights callous a friendship that God intends for extraordinary goodness.

I have this tendency, if I'm being perfectly real here, to assume others are as critical of me as I am of myself. I can imagine all kinds of rejection behind one brief conversation, 50 shades of judgment in a quick encounter, a brush-off around every corner.

But I have learned that the first step to clearing up a misunderstanding is to simply talk face to face with the other person. Usually a couple minutes of chitchat reveals how foolish I'm being. But on the rare occasion that I find the misunderstanding is not a figment of my imagination, going a little deeper in the conversation works wonders. Often times, the other person just needs to be heard, and I haven't given her my undivided attention. If I look her in the eyes and listen — actively, supportively listen — then she will likely tell me how I can be a better friend to her.

Talking in person and carefully listening solve the majority of misunderstandings. Rarely do those two steps not work. If they don't, it's usually because of one or both of the following reasons:

- one of us has suffered a deep hurt and needs help recovering, or
- one of us has decided to no longer love sacrificially.

As much as we wish we could be the agent of extraordinary change in our friend's life, we can't always be that friend to every person. Sometimes it's not God's plan to heal the wounds through us, and then the best thing we can do is to love from afar.

Fortunately, that is the rare exception. We notice the painful relationships because, well, the pain keeps reminding us. But in the vast majority of our relationships, we make connections and make a difference every day. It's true: *our ordinary reaching out makes extraordinary impact.*

And here is the truly extraordinary part — we have exponential influence. We each maintain several social circles. When you look at family, neighborhood, church, soccer teams, civic clubs, homeschool groups, PTAs, jobs, social media, and more — wow, we manage so many circles of friends! Each of our friends has several more circles. When we reach out and lift up one woman, she can minister more effectively to all those she touches. We touch infinitely more people with each relationship we nurture.

If you, my new friend, take anything away from this book, remember this: *you have extraordinary influence.* You can't see it, or measure it, or touch it, or even explain it, but every kind word to a cashier, every book read to a child, every verse repeated to a friend, every prayer you pray, every meal you make, every smile you share, ripples across countless circles of ordinary lives to make an extraordinary difference.

That is an amazing opportunity. And it's a grave responsibility. It's why we are commanded to love one another. God's plan for you is extraordinary, and you make a difference.

You just have to reach out.

What does the Bible say?

Read John 15 and Romans 12.

What does it mean to you?

Journal your answers and discuss with a friend.

1. Make a list of at least 100 people you impact on a regular basis. You may get stuck halfway through, but soon you'll realize you touch more lives than you thought!
2. Highlight those on your list that you need to reach out to more intentionally.
3. Take time to call or text each of those and schedule your next opportunity for face time.
4. List the different circles of influence you travel in — family, church, neighborhood, work, sports teams, clubs, etc. Are you developing relationships within each one? Where should you increase your efforts?
5. Pray over painful relationships that came to mind while you were reading this chapter. Have you given the hurt to God? Are you willing to let Him heal your friend without you?
6. What misunderstandings do you need to clear up? Schedule a face-to-face time when you can listen deeply and humbly.
7. Who do you know that underestimates her influence? How will you reach out to encourage her this week?

The Important People

Part II

To believe that our God never changes is to know that God will never change His relationship with us.

4

The Most Important Part

A chapter with such a title can only be about one thing, right? **Food.** Because eating is number one. I love to eat. I've been eating my entire life, several times a day, as though my very existence depended on it. Eating is one of my absolute favorites. And, eh-hem, it shows. So three or five or seven times a day, I make sure to set aside time for some good food. Maybe some *huevos rancheros* and coffee (of course, coffee!) in the morning; some warmed-up leftovers or a thick sandwich at noon; various fruit snacks and candies while I'm writing in the afternoon; a big, meaty stew or rich pasta sauce for dinner; and a cupcake or almond milk ice cream before bed.

Eating is not my problem; I'm really good at it after all this practice. But watching what I eat is a bigger issue. I have logged my eating choices and tracked my calories with some success, but stress or fatigue or a party gets me right back into the munching routine so fast that my diet app can't keep up.

So while I may think I'm always hungry, in truth I'm far from starving. That's what my bathroom scale reminds me constantly.

I wish I fed my spiritual life so generously, because truth be told, I stuff my face far more often than my soul. There's an urgency to mealtime, an ingrained habit to snacking that doesn't easily translate to the spiritual disciplines of prayer and Bible reading.

And I say that to my shame.

You know what? I'm taking a big risk by being honest about that, because it's much cooler to post a Bible meme on social media or a picture of my coffee mug with my devotional journal or to use trendy translations in Facebook statuses than to admit the harsh, human truth: *I didn't have devotions today.* Or worse, to honestly say, "I read through my daily Bible reading, but two hours later I had already forgotten every word of it. I raided the refrigerator twice in the same amount of time."

The fact of the matter is that this is a struggle we don't always win. It doesn't matter if we schedule Quiet Time early in the morning or during baby's naptime or late at night. It helps only moderately that we carry every translation known to mankind on our smart phones and purse-sized tablets and can listen to a devotional reading in the bathroom or in the car or in the kitchen. The gospel truth is *we're distracted.* All the time. And we hunger after all the wrong things.

Two thousand years after Christ urged us to hunger and thirst after Him, we remain distracted from the most important thing, and it's starving us spiritually — you and me, both.

I can recall times I was faithfully — almost monastically — devoted to Bible reading and prayer. Years when teenaged Lea Ann clung to the morning disciplines to obtain favor from a Heavenly God who seemed the most demanding, impossible-to-please parent of all; early adulthood's dark months of desperate clinging to the Psalms and pleading cries to a ceiling of brass for mercy, grace, and forgiveness from a depressing shame; the frantic Bible readings, Scripture memory, and repeated prayers through months of loneliness, pain, and loss. The lean years of trials and palpable soul-hunger that literally drove me to my arthritic knees in an attempt to win grace from the Almighty Deliverer.

When you're starving, you can think of nothing but food.

But just like our physical bodies can't live constantly in a crisis state, neither can our souls. That's why God brings relief from trials, provision for each day, and rest every night. "Weeping may endure for a night, but joy comes in the morning" (Psalms 30:5). When our cravings are satisfied, we are free to relax and notice our other blessings, other opportunities, other activities.

And then . . . we get distracted.

I don't know why my stomach clock is more consistent than my soul clock. I can't go but a few hours before my body reminds me that the refrigerator is full. But I could remain busy for days before realizing I'm behind on my Bible reading plan. There just isn't the same urgency.

Leaning on *the* Source

That's my fault for allowing myself to be distracted. I spend more time scrolling social media than searching the Scriptures. I complain about the weather more than I pray for souls. I "like" funny memes more than I praise the Creator. The disgusting truth is that I'm so full of the world's junk food that I've lost my appetite for healthy soul food.

Because I know in my brain and in my heart that nothing else will satisfy. I know that social media and TV and new clothes and better decorating and a heaping plate of beefy goodness will not satiate my seething desires. I know that no matter how large I grow on the scale, food and drink will not complete me — only God Himself can fill me up.

Only Scripture contains God's breathing, His very life force. Only God's Word gives me lasting value, knowledge, truth, protection, instructions, and purity. Only God's Word will fill me up and complete me, so that I can boldly face everything God wants me to do and to become (to paraphrase 2 Timothy 3:16–17). God intends my devotions to be just that — my heart turned devotedly back to my Creator.

Instead of feasting on the generosity of God's self, I swing in guilt to the other extreme, working hard, once more, for God's grace. Getting up earlier, kneeling on harder surfaces, using larger words in prayer, inwardly flagellating my own spirit in Protestant penance for my wayward spiritual life. The Almighty knows I deserve punishment. If I chastise myself first, then maybe my Heavenly Father won't have to.

Is that how Eve felt, that fateful day? Is that what she cried to herself while desperately trying to sew leaves thick enough to cover her ever-present shame? Is that why she hid her face from the only One who could save her from herself?

Then she pled *distraction.* It was the voice of that snake — she just couldn't escape it. Cursed serpent just couldn't stop reminding her of everything she wanted, everything she thought she didn't have, and everything she denied that she already was. Right in front of her face every day was literally everything she could ever desire, and she forgot what she wanted most of all.

All she ever wanted was significance, to be like God. Oh, the irony! She gave up everything to pay the ultimate price just to lose what she already had.

That's why the guilt trips don't lead to paradise. This struggle to stay in the light, to look up at His face, to listen to His still, small voice is the battle every daughter of God has wrestled with from the beginning of time. No human effort of our own — no scheduling, no smart phone app, no accountability group, no works of righteousness will set it right. As long as we blind our eyes to reality, glut ourselves on the fast food of the world, and listen to the lies around us, we will never truly find the communion and peace we seek. Instead, we're trapped in the cycle of distraction, desperation, guilt, depression, and self-condemnation.

That is never where God intends me and you to be. Look what He did for Eve — sacrificing for her, clothing her, promising redemption for her, loving her. God wants to do the same for us.

Building *the* Relationship That Matters

God sacrifices for our relationship with Him. He sought out Eve when He knew she was in sin, and He seeks us out to rescue us from our own condemnation. He spilled first the blood of animals and then *His very own perfect blood* to pay the just penalty for my wrong and yours. But that's not the end! Every day, God gives of Himself — leading us, wooing us, speaking to us, protecting us, providing for us. No matter what mistakes and trials the day holds, no matter how distracted and misdirected our efforts, God lovingly calls us back to Himself.

Then God clothed Eve so she could stand respectably before Him and before her family. Casting aside her poorly made, leafy garment, He fitted her in fine leather and fur. Now she was protected from the elements as well as from her shame in her designer, tailor-made ensemble. God is still dressing us in His armor today, suiting us for the spiritual engagements we face. The Almighty's own strength and power fit us for His calling and protects us from elements we may never realize.

God redeemed Eve, bought back her ruined existence for His own glory. Eve shouldered the terrible guilt of knowing she cursed her family, all of creation, and the entire human race. Yet she could praise God with each new child He gave her, knowing each baby embodied the physical manifestation of God's saving grace in her life — and ours. No matter our sin, no matter our inadequacies, no matter our distractions, God redeems our lives for His purposes, and those plans of God far exceed our wildest imaginations.

God's love for Eve never changed. As we read her tragic story, the one constant is *God Himself.* Everything changed for Eve that day when she took things into her own hands and then fled the scene of the crime. But God didn't change at all. He still loved her, He still sought her, *He still wanted her.* She was beautiful and desirable in His sight, because when He looked at her, He saw the image of His Son that would be redeemed in her.

God loves us that much. When we mess up, when we fall into sin, when we fail, when we are lost in the darkness, when we are distracted, when we lose hope and lose sight, God loves us the same. To believe that our God never changes is to know that *God will never change His relationship with us.*

I can't think of Eve without remembering her picture in my preschool storybook Bible. In dark, dismal greens and browns, the garden drooped as a sorrowful Adam and Eve clung to one another, heads bowed, trudging forlornly out of Eden. It is one of the saddest sights a four-year-old me could imagine. And the illustration still depicts the distraction/desperation/guilt/depression/self-condemnation cycle of our own spiritual lives.

But it's not the final scene.

Beginning with that slow walk of shame away from paradise, countless mothers, sisters, and friends brought their sacrifices, together with their children and their community, and looked ahead for God's perfect, loving, lasting redeeming provision. Generations later, one dark Friday, another mother looked on with horror and amazement as her Perfect Son paid the ultimate blood price for her own distracting, depressing guilt. And forever after, we are cleansed, clothed, and complete. Because of His sacrifice, the condemnation is gone!

This is our new life — a new relationship that transcends our condemnation, our depression, our guilt, our desperate grasping and striving, the ever-present distractions of this harried existence. God's love calls us back to that sacred relationship, to the power and peace only He can give.

God never intended *devotions* to be a guilt-inducing task on my to-do list. He is not pleased with Bible reading plans exalted in prideful hypocrisy. My relationship with Him is not measured in minutes on my knees or number of verses memorized. I will not achieve His pleasure through an app on my phone or a meme on my social media account. All these vanities miss the heart of the matter.

The Holy God didn't die for my knees or my eyes or my memory or my to-do list. He paid the price for *me,* for who I am and for who He wants to re-create me to be. He seeks me for my love, for my sincere relationship with Himself.

And that relationship changes everything.

The Almighty Creator of *everything* is mindful of just me — He knows every minute detail of every part of my day. He knows my mistakes and failings, He knows my hopes and dreams. He knows my busyness and worries and chores and recreation, and He just wants my love and worship through it all.

How can I help but adore Him?!

When I keep that in mind — when I set these truths in front of myself and meditate on the depths of grace behind it all — the cycle is broken. The distraction of media, the desperation for attention, the guilty shame, the melancholy depression, the loathing condemnation is all replaced with God's own self, the Comforter within. Now the hunger returns, and I realize I am starving, I'm famished for God's own person. Tasting His goodness each day, recalling His blessings He has in store for me, feasting on His bounteous provision with those around me only increases my appetite.

Now I'm driven back to my Creator. I'm searching His Word for *who He is* instead of what He can do for me today; I'm praying throughout the day in *praise for His goodness* instead of demanding His gifts; I'm resting in His Spirit instead of striving for His approval.

This, my dear friend, is the relationship you and I were created for. Indeed, this is the relationship those around us crave. That significance we seek is in His eye, clasped in the palm of His hand, safe in the arms of Jesus.

So this transforms our Scripture reading: we are building a relationship through intimacy with Him. We look for clues throughout Scripture: Why does He love me? How is God's love evident? How does God lead His loved ones? How do God's children display their love for Him? What more can I learn about the One who loves me so?

This transforms our prayers: we are building a relationship through intimate communication with Him. We look for ways to express our growing love: How can I worship Him? How do I put into words what He has done for me? What distractions, sins, and darkness cast a shadow on our communion? What truths about Him or about my life with Him am I struggling with? How can I love Him more?

This transforms our practice of devotion: we are building a relationship through *continual fellowship.* We look for His leading and listen for His voice throughout the day, learning to run to Him first when the distraction cycle begins. We are hungering and thirsting — not chastising and condemning — to possess more of Him and less junk.

I have family members who struggle with alcoholism. They crave the relief from stress, escape from their problems, release from responsibility that intoxication promises. Unfortunately, by giving themselves over to the control of alcoholic beverages, they gain more of all those problems: more stress, more problems, more consequences of irresponsibility, and greater shame.

God wants us to become addicted, instead, to Him. Rather than becoming intoxicated with wine, He calls us to abandon our inhibitions to the Holy Spirit. Consuming more of God's person, giving ourselves over to the control of the Spirit fills us up, satisfies completely, and produces spectacular results. Just take a look at Ephesians 5.

That word *control* trips us up, though. Every hour of every day we struggle to control: our to-do lists, our children, our husband, the family calendar, our time, our hair, our housekeeping, our weight. We are locked in a never-ending, desperate struggle to control the uncontrollable. But we can't — or won't — give it up, because just the appearance of progress for a few moments or even a day keeps us addicted to this self-control façade — the façade of failure, because it always, inevitably, crashes down.

God is calling us to give up control of our lives and instead to feed a new God-addiction. Allow the Holy Spirit to control our appetites, our desires, our dreams; to glut on Him, His Word, His Spirit every hour; to confess our need and flee to Him every hour for satisfaction. He promises that satisfaction, the provision we need each moment. And this addiction results in unmistakable changes. Everything changes — our words, our attitudes, our habits, our relationships.

Imagine for just a moment what an hour of your day today would look like if you were completely intoxicated with the Holy Spirit. If you were totally given over to God, how would your to-do list read? What would your reply to your children sound like? Where would you go? What would your voice sound like? How would your marriage change? How would your work improve? Would you be nearly unrecognizable?

What if we truly craved Christ more than a bottle? What if we yearned for the Word of God like we hunger for dinner? What if we turned to the power of prayer more often than coffee?

All around us, people are starving for this. They are famished for approval, for recognition, for provision, for healing, for deliverance, for significance. We want to help our loved ones, our friends, and our community, but it has to start with us.

We can't give them the hope we don't have. We can't point them to a relationship we don't know. We must first own it for ourselves.

As long as we walk this cursed world, we will always fight the distractions that start the cycle. The world, the devil, and our own weak flesh will continually work against our best intentions. But the Spirit within us draws us; the Son calls us; the Father welcomes us.

We are loved, we are clothed, we are significant. Each of us is extraordinary.

And it's all because of this, our most important, life-sustaining relationship.

What does the Bible say?

Read Genesis 2:1–4:2 and Psalm 139.

What does it mean to you?

Journal your answers and discuss with a friend.

1. What do you crave more than God? Be painfully honest and list all the things that your body and spirit long for on a daily basis.
2. Go back and examine your list. Beside each item, write down what it is that each idea, substance, or material thing gives you. Why do you seek these things?
3. This exercise may already be causing some guilt feelings to rise. Is that because some of these benefits you listed in #2 are things you should be seeking from God? Are you truly satisfied by them, or do you find yourself rushing for more?
4. At what part of the distraction cycle do you find yourself today?
5. Look carefully at James 1: 13–21. How is the distraction cycle similar to the temptation cycle? And how do the cures for each compare?
6. Think back to periods of time when you were most fervent in your relationship with God. What circumstances drove you to seek Him?
7. How can you purposefully remind yourself of the difference between *relationship* and *duty* in your personal relationship with God? What Scripture verses are particularly helpful?
8. When you were reading this chapter, who came to mind as needing a closer relationship with God? How can you demonstrate the vibrant, intimate relationship they can have in Him?

Our success is directly tied to our most intimate relationship.

5

Love, Leadership, and Marriage

I have marital problems.

I have to tell you the truth, because this book is about facing the truth in our own ordinary lives, and the naked truth is that my marriage is not all jelly beans and back rubs. It's also arguing and grumbling and disappointing and misunderstanding and stress.

My marriage breeds two types of problems: the loud kind and the scary kind.

The loud kind of problems multiply like dust bunnies, billowing forth with regularity. My husband and I are both emotionally volatile people, and we don't hold back when we disagree. Now, since the beginning of our marriage we have foreseen (or experienced) the dangers that our version of verbal shock-and-awe might pose, so we set some terms of engagement: we won't speak disrespectfully to each other; we won't use foul language; we won't lie; we won't use the *divorce* word; we won't air our grievances publicly; if we argue in the front of the children, we'll also settle the fight in front of them. We will hash things out, and we will find agreement if it kills us. Then we'll move on.

With nearly two decades of our own version of fair fighting under our belt, we are pros at it now. Even our most strenuous disagreements seldom last longer than 48 hours. We're both natural talkers, so we can cram a whole lot of discussion within a day or two, exhausting either the subject or ourselves until someone gives in.

These are the types of marital problems many of us experience . . . we just try to pretend that we don't. We act as though everything is perfect, and our laundry doesn't stink, but everyone knows that's a sham. Our children know it. Our spouse knows it. Our close friends know it. We just aren't honest about it. We don't usually answer, "Hi, how are you today?" with "Fine, I nearly won a war of words with my spouse on the way to church."

So that's why I'm going to start off this difficult chapter telling you the truth right up front: *I have marital problems.* Not every day, but frequently. And maybe one or two big ones a year. Because David and I are two real, sinful people who are sometimes selfish and tired and cranky and insensitive and inconsiderate. And he's Latino. And I have hormones.

Besides the frequently loud (and somewhat humorous) marital problems, there's a more sinister, silent marital emergency. That's only happened twice in two decades, and it scared me to death both times. It's the kind where you wake up one day to find yourself standing in the middle of the house wondering where your marriage went and where it is going. It's the kind where you are suddenly filled with cold dread at seeing where this road is leading . . . and it's not to Happily Ever After.

It's the kind where you say, "So this is what it feels like right before the end of all the hopes and dreams." It's the kind that looks like your worst nightmares have come true.

Our first nightmare dawned nearly a decade into our marriage. We were living separate lives under the same roof, straining beneath unbearable financial and ministry and health and parenting stress. My husband had lost more than one job, and the pressure of keeping his bilingual position as a very obvious immigrant in the affluent East Coast town flattened the optimism out of him. He worked two jobs — banking all day and loading UPS® trucks all night — to make ends meet for years on end until it literally broke his back. And still he kept working in excruciating pain right up until his back surgery.

Meanwhile, I homeschooled three little children, taught private lessons for 15 hours a week, and volunteered at the church and school next door for nearly 30 hours a week. We had a child who vowed aloud to never obey us, and he went two years straight proving his point regularly. Meanwhile, we lived in the parsonage during an acrimonious church split. The anger and criticism issuing from the building next door compelled me to pull the children inside, pull down the shades, and pull myself further into my shell. David and I had neither the time nor energy for more than a passing kiss in the doorway, and our hearts and bodies were starved for affection.

Our marriage was quickly going under as temptation loomed large and close. I began to build walls around myself, anxious to protect my heart and spirit from the criticism and demands all around me. In fatigue and fear, I shut out friends and even family members, pasting a façade of friendliness to hide my crumbling emotions. I could not control the painful people surrounding me, so I turned to what I thought I could control: my time and my tasks. Micromanaging my productivity and projects, I managed all intimate relationships right out of my life. That included my husband.

If I was less and less available at home, though, other women were more and more available in the workplace. David's successful move to banking center management caught the attention of not only financial executives, but also clients — lonely female clients impressed by the handsome, young, upwardly mobile banker with a sexy accent.

We were both in trouble, and my husband recognized the danger before I was willing to even talk about it. So he took the brave step of moving our family clear across the country within eight weeks. It took a few more weeks before we were even ready to talk about what happened, what went wrong, how we had hurt each other, how *we nearly lost it all for what we didn't even want.*

How to Fix It

That brave man risked everything — our family security, our future, our home, his job, our spiritual lives, our hopes and dreams — to save what was *our most important human relationship.* Because none of those other things mattered if we lost each other.

And it paid off. God gave us everything we left behind and way, way more besides within the next couple of years. But even if He hadn't, we would have given everything to save our marriage.

When, a decade after that, we found ourselves again standing on opposite sides of a chasm of misunderstanding and loneliness and fear and hurt, we knew what to do. He left work in the middle of the day, and I put aside my ever-important to-do list, and we ran away from the house full of children to solve the most pressing problem of all: *why were we no longer one.* We talked over lunch; we meandered quietly through a couple of stores. Finally, we locked ourselves in the minivan right there in the parking lot to cry hot tears of desperation, fighting together for the truth in our relationship. We asked each other the hard questions and listened with courage. We took turns pointing out *where we went wrong,* and we took turns forgiving. Within four hours, we found each other again, repairing the brokenness between us.

David and I both come from broken homes. Though our parents' marriages dissolved for different reasons and in different ways, we both came away from those experiences with the scarred reality that no marriage — no matter how long or affluent or religious or enviable — *no marriage is safe.* Every family is under attack every day.

We all have marital problems. We fight, we argue, we hurt, and we complain. We struggle with finances, sickness, children, housing, jobs, and in-laws. We battle fatigue, loneliness, misunderstanding, stress, and fear. We have problems — but it's what we do with the problems that counts.

Since we knew from the beginning we were going to have problems, my husband and I decided that we would fight together for the solutions to those problems. That's the key: we are going to fight. Marriage often feels like a battle. And sometimes it looks like we are fighting each other. But in our hearts we know we are fighting together for the solution, and we won't stop until we both win.

That means even two loud fighters like us need to *listen* a lot. I need to make sure I hear what the problem is from his perspective since I'm pretty consumed with my own ideas. I need to listen actively: asking questions, repeating back what I heard him say, putting more energy into understanding him than into pushing my own viewpoint. That is probably the hardest part for me.

I also need to be completely honest. That is painful, because when I am hurting, I won't talk. Instead, I want to pull all the pain and wounds close within me, shutting out everyone and everything around me in self-preservation mode. But that shuts out the one person I need most. Intimacy will grow and wounds will heal when I expose them to the light, when I open up to the truth.

But this takes a lot of time, a lot of back-and-forth of listening and exposing, asking questions and answering honestly. The process becomes painful, tearful, even fearful, until we both wrestle out the problem together. Then we are finally ready to solve it. After we have both named the problem and agreed on what it is, we usually see the solution fairly quickly. We then can brainstorm several solutions and find one that fits us both well.

However, we aren't done just yet. It's tempting to just slap a bandage on the problem and rush off to our regularly scheduled busy lives, but that's not going to make us one again. Instead, we need to take time to remember our dreams, to reframe them with the solutions we just prescribed. We need to say, out loud, to each other what this solution makes possible and how achieving it together makes our long-term dreams for our marriage a reality.

We need to stay there, wrestling the problem and solution into our Together Dreams, until the dreams become reality in our relationship, the common course we are both on together, the irresistible future we are traveling toward hand-in-hand.

Then the conversation, of course, goes toward how we will achieve those dreams — what we are doing now, this week, this month, this year, this stage in our lives to achieve what we *know* God created our togetherness for.

Now you see why our fights take so long. We have a lot of ground to cover! But when we take the time, the sweat, the tears to walk that journey together, we find ourselves more at *one* than ever before. Walking out of Eden together, toward the future of redemption and promise.

When a marriage relationship is built on that unity, fighting and hugging and all, the issue of leadership is no longer at odds with biblical submission. Every day, every decision, every fight, every make-up session is all about Ephesians 5: *Submitting yourselves one to another in the fear of God.* We listen to each other, we expose truth to each other, we cast visions for each other, we plan for fulfillment with each other, we forgive, we give, we hug, we serve, because we honor God within each other. Husbands were not created for us wives, but we wives for them (1 Corinthians 11:9). But those men aren't so good without us (Genesis 2:18). We *complete each other* in the awe-inspiring plan of God for two to be one. So we each submit, yielding ourselves to the unity of redemption.

In spite of the world's clamor for women to achieve more, be more, do more, in reality *our success is directly tied to our most intimate relationship.* What we are in secret is what we are in public, and what we are in our bedroom is what we are in church. We cannot achieve more in God's economy than we are willing to sacrifice inside our own sacred home.

That's easier said than done. After a day of work, housework, cooking, running errands, homeschooling, and child-rearing, we can feel depleted, uninspired, and even needy. It is ever-tempting to put public service (with its accolades, gratitude, and recognition) ahead of private servitude. But *servitude* isn't a bad word — it's the goal. It's Christ-likeness.

Herein lies the struggle. When we put our marriage first, valuing intimacy over acclaim, matrimony over money, relationship over reward, we actively oppose everything our world, our flesh, and our enemy tell us every single day. We fight against the lie of Eden, that we have to make ourselves into a goddess instead of serving the man standing right beside us. But God calls us to put down the fruit and come to the altar.

True leadership and lasting influence, isn't about glass ceilings or salaries or awards or titles. It's about intimacy and unity — first with God, then with our man. These priorities don't mean we won't ever manage or own or achieve, but we must change our perspective. We need to look closely at who we are as revealed in the mirror of intimacy, because that image of Christ and our marriage indicates what we are replicating in others. I am no better leader than I am follower of Christ and lover of my husband.

I frequently get into trouble when I rush ahead of my husband in decisions. Like Eve rushing into fruit selection, I'm pretty sure I know what's right and that my man will be so grateful I made the choice for him. But by neglecting to seek unity in decision-making, my foolishness can easily make a mess of things and even cause harm to those around me.

Don't get me wrong — women are great decision-makers. Many of the smartest people I know are women, and I'm no slouch, myself. But we easily forget that *we are only half of the solution.* That guy next to me isn't just eye candy — he is the answer. That's why family decisions, childrearing problems, ministry opportunities, and plans, hopes, and dreams must be conceived and realized in unity together. I am only half of the equation. The solution is unity.

When we seek unity, we also find the support we crave. Suddenly, we aren't alone in the struggle, but instead we have an ally. And as we support his authority inside and outside the home, uphold his dreams for his future and for his family, and communicate our desire for his best, we find the same for ourselves.

As women, we think of leadership as something we do *out there,* as what strangers and coworkers and church members and community members know us for. But radical, world-changing, extraordinary leadership is intimacy, and it starts with our own marriage. Our ordinary marriage. One regular woman and her heartthrob husband who set aside regular date nights and lunch meetings and weekends away to keep the fires burning. A plain Mr. and Mrs. who text and email and call and chat about love and laundry, dinner and dreams, bills and beliefs.

That kind of love can change the world.

What does the Bible say?

Read 1 Corinthians 7; Hebrews 13:1–18.

What does it mean to you?

Journal your answers and discuss with a friend or your spouse.

1. If you are unmarried, consider this chapter's discussion of intimacy and unity in light of 1 Corinthians 7:25–40. How does intimacy with God strengthen your ministry and leadership?
2. Of the two kinds of marital problems discussed, which are you currently facing? Make an appointment with your spouse to practice the solution strategy outlined in this chapter.
3. When was the last time you and your spouse discussed your dreams together? Are you both clear on your goals for now and for the future? What does a happy marriage look like to you?
4. What decision are you facing? Have you talked it over with your husband?
5. What area of your life could use more support? Have you communicated to your spouse what support is most meaningful to you?
6. Where does your husband need more support? What kind of support does he say is most meaningful?
7. What leadership opportunities outside the home do you have? List work, ministry, school, and community organizations you influence. Set aside time with your spouse to discuss each one. Share your vision for each area of influence the Lord has given you and listen carefully to your husband's insights.
8. List meaningful ways you can demonstrate to your husband that your marriage is your priority relationship.

Ordinary
parenting requires
extraordinary faith
and grace.

6

Raising Leaders

The hardest part about raising my four children is the apologizing. I swear, I hardly get my coffee poured in the morning before I have to apologize to one of them for a cross word or misunderstanding. Or for stepping on their toy and breaking it. Or for checking out a book on their library card and getting them a big fine. Or for accusing them of not cleaning their room when it was really a sibling that needed the scolding. Just while writing this chapter, I've had to apologize twice.

It seems like I spend half the day correcting the wrong child and the other half of the day apologizing. Meanwhile, I'm juggling laundry from piles on the floor to machines to piles on beds, and shuffling stacks of homeschool papers from desk to desk, and running late to appointments.

This does not, on the surface, appear to be the way to train the leaders of the next generation, but I'm here to tell you, my friend, that it is the only way to do just that. Stumbling and apologizing and trying again is the only way to parent.

Everyone knows how to be the perfect mother until she has to sleep-train her infant or potty-train her toddler. Then, suddenly, the best laid plans and best-selling manuals fly out the door with weeping and wailing and soiled carpets. Those first two years of parenting teach us the age-old truth: you can have a perfect child, or you can have a real, human being child. You can't have both. Since we do not choose to invest ourselves in robots, we are stuck with the regular human children.

So we try teaching them to *obey*, and that's so important, because it's biblical, after all. And our grandparents are very pro-obedience, so there's the family pressure. And we experience those raised eyebrows and clicking tongues at church, don't forget. So we roll up our sleeves and set our progeny on the sofa for the *big talk* about what God and mommy expect from short people who share our last name. There's even homework; I swear that by the age of two each of my own could repeat from memory *"Children, obey your parents in the Lord for this is right."*

Tantrums from a Toddler

Right from the beginning, my own firstborn rose up in rebellion against what seemed to me like a perfectly reasonable request: just do what I tell you to do. I even gave bonus points if he would also smile and say, "I love you, Mommy" while he was doing it. Such a reasonable request. But before he was even two years old, he had the audacity to step right up to me, wave a tiny fist in the air, and declare, "I will not obey you today, Mommy."

At first I was pretty sure I had misunderstood him, but no, he repeated his declaration of war. Then he proceeded to demonstrate his intentions every way he could find. Sandwiches, soldiers, and shirts went flying through the air. Dishes and rules were broken daily, along with the peace of our small family. There was a new despot in the house, and he barely reached my knee.

Either I was going to lose my religion, or he would give up his belief in tyranny. I resolved to never allow a toddler to overthrow the natural order of the family; but if I took his statement as a personal challenge, he even more so. The battle lines were drawn — in every room of the house. We fought over whether or not he would pick up his toys, whether or not he would put on pants, whether or not he would eat his sandwich, whether or not he would attend Sunday school, whether or not he would punch his friends. Basically, anything his parents told him to do, the answer was an unequivocal, "No. You can't make me." In those exact words. I daily regretted ever having taught him to speak.

My husband and I were resolute. No temper tantrums, no flying toys, no shaking fists, no tearful pleas would dissuade us — we would continue being the parents whether or not he wanted to be a good child. Even though, quite frankly, we no longer wanted to be the parents at this juncture. How sorely that boy tested my conviction. Was obedience *really* that important? Was it unreasonable to expect a toddler to put his parents' instructions ahead of his own desires? Or was I rearing a fresh, new juvenile delinquent?

But you know what I discovered when I talked to my mommy friends? Most of them had the same struggle with their firstborn child. There was no reason, in those puny little psyches, that the taller people absolutely had to be in charge. Perhaps the adults could be overthrown with some well-placed Duplo, far-flung soggy diapers, and sheer persistence.

The adults had to be *more* persistent: persistent in boundaries, persistent in consequences, persistent in love, persistent in consistency. And persistent consistency is exhausting.

My young terrorist was nearly successful in his rebellion, too. After a good two years of non-stop warfare over *every single request* his dad or I made, he finally exhausted himself. And soon after that, his sister started her own experiments with rebellion while her preschool-aged brother watched in smug amusement. Thankfully, the next two boys apparently learned from the mistakes of their older siblings and barely gave us a fight. At long last, the peasants were brought under subjection. We were, indeed and not only in name, the parents — large and in charge.

I would never like to live through The Great Toddler Rebellion of '01 again. I'm too tired now. Yet more parenting struggles rise before us: puberty, teen years, and the struggles for independence. I see no decade of *Pax Parenting* in my future.

When I see another mom struggling to quell her own offspring's uprising, I want to hand her a coffee and the Book of Psalms and remind her that it won't last forever. It can't — God promises we will reap *if we faint not.*

> Be not deceived; God is not mocked: for whatsoever a man soweth, that shall he also reap. For he that

> soweth to his flesh shall of the flesh reap corruption; but he that soweth to the Spirit shall of the Spirit reap life everlasting. And let us not be weary in well doing: for in due season we shall reap, if we faint not (Galatians 6:7–9; KJV).

We nearly faint with exhaustion, with worry, with discouragement during the tough parenting seasons. We bruise our knees with prayer and wrinkle our faces with tears and grey our hair with frustration over the spiritual battles waged every day.

And what, exactly, are we praying and working and sowing and teaching and hoping to reap if not *a life yielded to God's control,* a heart softened to the gentlest moving of the Spirit?

The battle for obedience is, in fact, the battle for the child's very soul. That is the extraordinary change we desire in this young, miniscule miscreant: the change from an ordinary baby, child, and teen to an extraordinary servant of God, yielded to Christ-like change in his own life and in the lives of those around him. A young one who grows in grace to influence those around him for God. A child obedient to his parents, so he will also submit to God.

Thus, ordinary parenting requires extraordinary faith and grace. First we sow faith, because we will not always see the harvest we plant. We don't see it that day; we may not see it that year. We may diligently teach and enforce, train and explain for years before the soil turns fertile and the son turns afresh to Christ. We know not the date of the *due season,* so we faint not; we faith it up until God shows up in the young life.

Then we liberally apply the fertilizer of grace. This hot, new buzzword in Christian discipline differs greatly from permissiveness or protection for consequences. Biblical grace is so much more: more love, more long-suffering, more truth. We measure out grace for our children because God pours out grace to us. *And He does* — freely, generously, and over-abundantly over the nothing we deserve and the leniency we desire.

God's grace, we must never forget, came to mankind after His standard of righteousness was set forth. Eve had already felt the penalty of her sin before grace was applied, and she had to come face-to-face with the judgment that her disobedience deserved before she could even begin to appreciate the grace willingly handed to her.

Grace That Grows

That's why one of the beautiful privileges of parenting children who have learned obedience is increasing grace. As children grow older, and hopefully a little bit wiser, they begin to experience less parental discipline and more natural consequences of their own wrong choices . . . and ever increasing grace.

Our children learn obedience, comprehend grace, and then find meaning. They observe our sincere walk with God and begin to appreciate the journey toward significance in Christ. They find their identity in Him because they watch our yielding to His will. Our sons know their work matters because their father's job is his ministry. Our daughters know relationships influence others because their mother's mission is to impact those around her. When we find our purpose in our Creator, our own children see life's purpose every day. All is God's glory.

This is the true challenge of raising leaders — *they see us as we really are.* My children observe my muttering over the chores, they hear the words I say when I step on a Lego, they see the look on my face when the phone rings for the fifth time that hour. They know how I *really* spend my time. They see my failures every day. Hence, the constant apologizing.

This is the hardest, most exhausting facet of discipleship — walking and sitting and eating and sleeping and living every single hour in full view of our intimate audience. It's the horrific reality of Deuteronomy 6: *our children will know the truth.* We cannot live and worship any other way but in full view of our children.

They will see the truth, and the truth will set them free. The truth of Christ's love, the experience of living for His glory is super-abundant liberation — free indeed (John 8:31–36). My husband and I endeavor, as much as lies within us, to model that truth before our children every day — not just living out the truth, but even speaking forth the truth with open sincerity — telling the truth about our mistakes, the truth about the mistakes of others, the truth about details of our lives big and small, the truth about the Bible and the world and creation and the news and the neighbors. Our children must know that no matter what happens, at least we are *honest* with them.

We parents often fear honesty with our children. We are afraid of what might happen if they know the truth about our failings, the truth about our fears, the truth about how much we really know and all the things we don't know, the truth about how much sin and danger is around them. Parenting in faith compels us to shine brightly the light of truth. Sharing that truth with our children allows them to grow in faith and grace as they learn to depend on God's Word and walk in His way. Faith-filled truth, boldly declared to our children and lived before them, is the surest shelter we can provide.

It's that openness that made even that oft-dreaded preteen *talk* surprisingly easy for me. From our earliest parenting years, we have always answered our children's questions honestly and straightforwardly. This openness set a comfortable foundation for even talking about the most personal, private information. Both of my oldest two actually came to me, in their own way, with questions about what makes babies and how the baby "gets inside there," and hardly anyone blushed to talk on the sofa in the living room or around the counter in the kitchen about the fun and sacred way God designed for parents to enjoy oneness. No one hesitated to talk about the remarkable transformation young bodies experience as they change from babies to young children to young adults. Young people fully accustomed to not only hearing God's Word read aloud regularly and discussing its application throughout the day find it natural that God ordained specific consequences for misusing his gift of marriage; they naturally understand and even expect consequences to individuals and families and entire communities when God's plan is violated.

So when my middle son didn't initiate the conversation in the usual way, I opened it up confidently myself. "You have grown up a lot this year, and I think you are man enough to know this information and handle it maturely." Just like I regularly pray that I am mature enough to guide my young men and woman into confident Christian adulthood, I sensitively answered his questions. I want him, as well as his brothers and sister, to always know he can talk to me and to his dad about anything, no matter how sensitive or private. The greatest protection from error is the truth. That's why we parents must seize the power of these critical conversations. Rather than dreading the awkward talks, we should welcome every opportunity to increase the trust, openness, and intimacy in our relationship with our young person.

These bold conversations teach our children that the truth is open, not hidden. When the truth is freely offered, the crude jesting and lewd jokes and juvenile misinformation from neighborhood kids or the locker rooms or the workplace break rooms hold little fascination. And when we elevate the truth, it becomes a privilege to bear it, to protect it, to live it boldly.

Parenting is imparting truth, passing the inheritance of God's grace-filled, loving truth to the next generation. Then when childhood obedience to parental truth yields softly over time to bolder honesty and grace, the young teen approaches adulthood's freedom with truth's shining light illuminating the difficult road toward independence. We can confidently cheer our young men and women forward in their journey of faith knowing God will be glorified in their lives.

Faith through Failure

Parenting in truth requires faith through our failures. The truth cannot be hidden from our teens. They see us with increasing clarity. As their mothers, we must come to terms with our own inadequacies, because they are no longer hidden from our family. You see, our failures as mothers don't lose the battle for the hearts and souls of our children. Our hypocrisy does. The problem is not our mistakes; it is our vain attempt to cover them up. It is not our humanity, but our disregard for the God-image within us and within them. We don't have to be perfect parents, praise God, but we must be sincere. God calls us to be ordinary moms who boldly live the truth.

And what if our child chooses to walk away from that truth? What if our own son or daughter rebels against God? Does this, then, mean that our labor *was* in vain, and that all our faith and efforts and prayers were to no effect? God forbid! That honest choice we made in the garden of our own heart to turn from sin to the

Savior must be afforded our own child, and he must stand on his own feet before God, fearful though that prospect may be. It would be dishonest of us to make the choice for him, because he, too, must appear before God on his own. We can point our child to the Cross, but we cannot make him eat of the Bread of Life and drink of the cup of Christ. We can only watch and pray in faith.

We continue to pray and apologize and give grace and seek grace and love and sacrifice and wait with expectation that someday — not the day we expect, not the way we expect — but someday we shall indeed reap if we faint not.

My teen interrupted my writing today for help on his college entrance essay. His topic was to be spiritual leadership, which he found daunting. "I'm not a *leader,* Mom! I'm just a friend, someone to support my friends and listen to them and help them the best I can to be the best they can be." Tears came to my eyes as the ironic truth became clear — isn't that, fellow mommy, what our influence at home is truly all about? Being friends and counselors and support and direction to our young ones so that they can grow and do the same for those around them? My son didn't realize that was Christ's definition of a leader, and maybe you forget some days, too. But you are changing lives — one truth at a time.

What does the Bible say?

Read Ephesians 6 and James 1.

What does it mean to you?

Journal your answers and discuss with a friend or your spouse.

1. If you do not have children, how does this chapter's emphasis on obedience, grace, and honesty apply to your ministry toward children or even your life in the workplace?
2. What stage of life are each of your children in? List each one, and consider their growth in relation to obedience, grace, and truth.
3. What specific ways could you use to teach your child greater obedience?

4. Does your parenting tend toward *strict obedience* or *overabundant grace*? What are the strengths and weaknesses of your own parenting habits?
5. Is it painful or easy for you to speak truth habitually to your children? Make a note for one week every time you are tempted to exaggerate, hedge, or hide the truth in matters big or small. Begin a habit of apologizing and uncovering the truth for them each time.
6. When was the last time you apologized to your child? Did you make excuses, blame the child, or otherwise turn from a sincere admission of guilt? Is there something you need to apologize for now?
7. Is your child wrestling with his relationship with God? How can you model intimacy with Christ in your own obedience, grace, and truth?

The painful parts

Part III

God's grace never flows the way we imagine, but it always fills God's perfect plan for our family history.

7

Misshapen Homes

Twenty years ago, my parents disowned me.

It's probably not the story you'd expect from a homeschool graduate and deacon's kid. But it's the truth. After 19 years of physical and emotional abuse and a year of unsuccessfully pleading for help, I took my safety into my own hands, ran away, and eloped. In retaliation, my parents cut me off from themselves and from my grandparents, from my friends and my church, from everyone I knew.

Obviously, it took a few years to rebuild relationships after that. I had to learn how to start over with a new family, new community, new church, new relationships everywhere. It was the loneliest, darkest road I will ever walk.

I still struggle two decades later to even think about that period of my life. I rarely whisper about it with my closest friends, and I've never written a word about it before now. I feel compelled to share a tiny bit of my journey, though, because I sense you may have experienced a similarly painful experience. Perhaps you are walking a valley yourself right now, and I never want you to think that you are alone.

The first two decades of my life pained my spirit. But beyond the beatings, the public and private shaming, the tongue lashings and cursings, the humiliating confusion of growing up abused, I think the most devastating part was the *isolation*. I always felt so painfully alone — alone in my classroom, alone in my Sunday school, alone in my family. No one knew what was really going on. My friends didn't understand how my family was different, teachers couldn't comprehend my mood swings, and adults couldn't imagine (or didn't want to believe) the double lives my family members were living as upstanding church members protecting secret sin. I had no words to explain it, no way to communicate what I was dealing with, no perspective to understand my situation, no comprehension of what was *right* and what was *wrong* inside my family. Even in the few moments when, in a flash of realization, I saw the difference between the painful, twisted relationship I had with my parents in comparison with the loving homes of my friends, there was no way I could speak up. I had no voice in my reality.

Then when I was out of the situation, on my own and without any extended family at only 19 years old, I felt like I still had no support and no way to explain my loneliness. I remember when my husband and I were expecting our first child, one of the first things coworkers would ask is, "When is your mother coming to see the baby?" I would awkwardly stand there, fighting back the tears, trying to figure out how to explain that I have a mother, but I don't really have a Mom anymore.

The birth of my first child remains the most wonderful and the most painful day of my life. I remember holding his surprisingly plump, rounded perfection, eight and a half pounds swaddled in pink-and-blue striped hospital blankets; his off-the-charts enormous, perfectly round head and the nursery's matching striped newborn cap seeming as though it were made for smaller, lesser babies half his size. For the first time, the wonder of becoming a mother hit me with fierce terror. I was to become the parent — a station in life that held no attraction for me. Would I grow to hate this lovely creation, and would I spend his life instilling fear into his very soul?

So after my best friend bounded into the delivery room to congratulate and hug me, after my gregarious mother-in-law departed to broadcast the news across two continents, my husband left to call the rest of his family and to leave a message on my father's answering machine. So I was alone in the room when the phone rang. "Hi,

Lea. I got your message. Congratulations." The sound of his voice — so familiar, yet so far away — brought sharp pain stronger than my delivery drugs could assuage. He asked if I had counted all the fingers and toes, and I shared length and weight and name — cold, objective facts to mask the fresh wounds. Focusing on the clean, white ceiling above me, I practiced my deep labor breathing to stay calm. We spoke in stilted voices through the poor connection across the thousands of miles, hundreds of hurts, years of wounded spirits and crushed dreams, until he passed the phone to his new fiancé, and then my sister, and then it was over. I hung the heavy phone back in its cradle and buried my face, my anguish, my unspoken screams in the thin maternity pillows, wondering if and when my mother would ever know her grandson was born, and if she would even care.

I had no family to hand my first baby to. I was an orphan mother, an abandoned mommy. What should have been the happiest moment of my life was shadowed by the unanswerable wail of my heart, "WHY? Why don't you love me? Why would you intentionally hurt and purposefully discard your own daughter? How could a Christian family no longer care about their own?"

Somewhere deep inside, I had wondered if becoming a mother myself would help me see the problem from their perspective, but instead I found myself further perplexed.

Some Questions Have No Answers

There was — there is — no answer to those questions.

As I learn to live with the unanswerable, I find many women live with similarly inexplicable pain. Almost everyone I know has painful people — loved ones who behave unlovingly or who are downright unlovable: wayward children, meddlesome in-laws, critical parents, or prodigal siblings. We are burdened for unsaved relatives and close friends who deliberately make the same wrong choices again and again. We grieve over the hypocrisy of others who claim to know Christ but don't live His clear command to love.

We carry these burdens alone, remaining isolated by our pain and further isolating ourselves against being painfully uncovered, hiding the wounds in shame and fear.

It took years of counseling from friends and clergy members before I could even begin to recognize healing. Like many victims of childhood abuse, I had to learn to function in an entirely new reality than the one I had grown up in, and I had to begin that process well before I could rebuild lost relationships. So in case you are from a similarly broken or misshapen home, if perhaps you struggle relating to painful people, here is a plan for help.

Accept That Much of Your History Is a Lie

What you thought was fact was a fabrication, what you were told was true was a cover-up, and what you thought was normal was actually unnatural. Not all of it, but even the true parts are mixed up with the lies, so you have to start from scratch. This is actually hard to accept; the most common way children preserve their relationships is through denial. Even after leaving home, I refused to admit there was anything wrong with my family for nearly three years later. *Admitting there is a wrong is the first step toward healing.*

Make Yourself Tell the Truth Ruthlessly

If you were a victim of childhood abuse, *lying was how you survived.* You lied to your teachers about why you had bruises, you lied to your friends about how happy you were, you lied to yourself about what really happened behind closed doors. Lying is such a habit that you don't recognize when you are doing it, so you need to hold yourself accountable — and ask those around you to hold you accountable. When you do lie, immediately apologize and say the truth. Continually pray that God will show you the truth, give you the strength to say it, and forgive you for lying. As you cling to the truth and eschew the lies, God will develop within a love for His truths and the freedom they bring.

Find Safe Friends

Your spouse needs to hear the whole truth from you; your closest, bestest friend needs to hear the whole truth from you; and your pastor needs to hear the whole truth from you. Make sure each of those is a safe person: someone who loves you and your truth and commits to seeing God's best purpose worked in your life. Be transparent in your words and actions before your safe friends, trusting them with the truth of your healing journey so they can pray for you, support you, counsel you, and protect you while you recover. Having two or three people to love you through recovery is invaluable, and the more honest you are the faster you will heal.

Who are these safe people? Not everyone you meet should be entrusted with your hurt, and not everyone around you should be exposed to your raw wounds. The right people are out there — you just need discernment to identify them. You will recognize your safe people by these characteristics:

- They are characterized by love for others.
- They not only refrain from gossip, criticism, and tale-bearing, but they avoid those who do.
- They are loyal friends, maintaining friendships over years and miles.
- They have a close, intimate walk with God that affects every aspect of their life.
- They know God's healing power over their own broken past and rejoice in the new life the Lord has given them.
- They sacrifice for their loved ones, maintaining relationships with their spouse, grown children, and childhood friends through thick and thin.
- They take personal responsibility for their own failings, and they are quick to forgive others.
- They never use relationships to exalt their own standing but rather seek to serve.
- They keep close confidence, pray faithfully, and rejoice in God's care.

Re-examine

Re-examine what you believe, who you are, what your past included, and what your future holds.

During the puberty and the teen years, young people settle many of these issues while "finding themselves." A young woman decides if she will follow her family's religion, what principles she will use to guide her life, how she determines right and wrong, and how she measures success. She will ascertain who she is and how she describes herself, how she reacts to conflict, and what strengths she will develop. She internalizes her own personal history and merges it into her own story of where she will go and what she will do as an adult.

But for the abused child, this process is warped, because most of the conclusions she came to are built on deceit. So, as adults recovering from traumatic childhood, we need to work through all those issues again. This feels very, very scary; most teens wrestle with these issues from within the protection of parental guidance and rules, so they can test their beliefs in a safe environment with loving support. As an adult, we find ourselves suddenly working without a net while questioning the very tightrope we stand on.

I remember my horror one day at the age of 20 as I looked down at my Bible at the very verses therein used to justify beating me, cursing me, and casting me aside, and suddenly wondered, *Is all this wrong? Is anything true?* The sunny Florida sky outside my apartment belied the thick clouds that rolled into my heart as I cast the Good Book aside and myself to the floor in sobbing despair at a life that meant nothing apart from the Heavenly Father who had kept me sane through my painful years growing up.

I entered a deep depression, rocking myself on the floor in our nearly empty apartment for days on end, unable to work or sleep or communicate my despair at the prospect of a life without meaning, without the One who had held my mind and spirit together for two decades. It was days before I could find the words to express my fear and disillusionment to my husband. It took me weeks more to enter, warily, a church building, and months to open the leather cover of my Bible. With time and the gentle patience of my husband along with the loving encouragement of my friend, I slowly began to disentangle *hypocritical man* from the truth of God's Word. Then later I could move forward to *what really happened at home?* and even *does God have a plan for me?*

Take Your Time

There were times during my recovery journey that I was desperate, *truly desperate,* to see the truth immediately, to know healing, to feel peace. But only God can mend a sinner's heart, and He often uses a long passage of time. How many years did God keep Joseph's brothers away from Egypt before reuniting them? How long must those 40 years of healing and resting in the wilderness have seemed to the twice-orphaned Moses? How many years until Sarah could forgive her husband Abraham's betrayals and learn to trust him again? Healing may be measured not in months but in decades. But in time we can — surely we can — see gradual change over each successive year.

Cling to Your Father in Heaven

> Sing unto God, sing praises to his name: extol him that rideth upon the heavens by his name JAH, and rejoice before him.
>
> A father of the fatherless, and a judge of the widows, is God in his holy habitation.
>
> God setteth the solitary in families: he bringeth out those which are bound with chains (Psalm 68:4–6; KJV).

I can look back now through my childhood and clearly see that *God was there.* The intimacy in my childhood's frantic early-morning devotions assured me He was with me; His presence when I knelt in my basement in prayer comforted my spirit; the peaceful sleep that came when I cried out to Him on my pillow at night showed me He knew my needs. As a young girl, I never doubted that God loved me, because every day *He walked with me and He talked with me* in a close, intimate fellowship I've never known since, but I eagerly look forward to in heaven.

Know God Has a Plan

One cold Michigan Sunday, I visited my childhood church with my young son. In a crowded hallway, an older lady grabbed me (physically held me by the arms), and looked earnestly into my face. "I need to tell you, Lea Ann, that God is not done with you.

Your life is just beginning, and God has an amazing purpose for you. Satan will tell you that you are ruined, that your life is too broken, that you are worthless. But that's a lie. The truth is that *you are valuable to God, and He is using you and will continue to work His will through you.* Don't ever doubt that, and don't ever turn away from that truth."

I sobbed in front of her, and I have never, *never* forgotten her words. They are for you, too.

One of the most remarkable and redeeming parts of our healing story, friend, is that God uses you and me in spite of our past pain, that God can actually use us as agents of hope and healing in the midst of our misshapen families. Like our own healing, this ministry of love doesn't happen on our timetable. God's grace never flows the way we imagine, but it always fills God's perfect plan for our family history.

Can we become brave enough, bold enough, and brilliant enough to shine light into the dismal dismay of our misshapen homes? I know God delights to do just that, because He miraculously mended my heart to that of my mother in His own glorious purpose.

Perhaps you despair of ever being reconciled to that wayward family member, or maybe you are struggling with a difficult relationship. Here is how God both protected me and worked out a beautiful reconciliation.

Set Protective Boundaries

Before we can renew broken relationships, we must first be clear about God's will for our own lives. God's loving plan for us always includes our physical, emotional, and spiritual well-being. Before we can share healing with others, we must first become healthy ourselves. That is why *protective boundaries* are so important. The roadmap I shared with you above — the healing process for deep, intimate hurt — must be journeyed in a safe environment. In my case, I moved to the other side of the country from everyone who wished me harm, far enough away that no one could hurt me or even contact me without considerable effort. My husband kept close tabs on where I was at all times, and the local police were notified of harassing contact in case things escalated. We lived in a secure, gated community, so I didn't worry about someone showing up unannounced.

When my physical protection was secured, we could move on to my emotional protection. We installed an answering machine (this was before mobile technology) so we could screen phone calls, and eventually I turned the volume all the way down on the machine and the ringer off the phone so I would not hear the phone ring and become afraid. My husband took in the mail and threw harassing and upsetting letters in the dumpster before I ever saw them. My in-laws, church leaders, and employers were instructed to contact my husband, not me, if anyone out of state requested my personal information or attempted to contact me.

Then my husband set out to provide for my *spiritual* protection. He began reading from the Bible each day aloud to me, gentle devotionals to renew my trust in God's Word. He dragged me, reluctantly, to church services, after first calling ahead to make sure the service environment would be gentle for my fragile state. He prayed for me in front of me, reminding me that God intended for my healing and my ultimate good.

So when family members eventually *did* seek out reconciliation, my husband took the front line, speaking with them individually first to determine if that was the right time to reconnect. Because he took the initiative protecting me and shielding me, I was prepared when reconciliation began.

So if you are hurting, be sure to take the first step of protection. Find a safe person — your spouse, your pastor, or a close friend — who can clearly and decisively draw a boundary around your body, heart, and spirit. Then you can peacefully take the afore-mentioned steps of healing while trusting God to deal with the other parties.

Hold to the Truth

My reconciliation with my mother took years, and truth was the biggest issue. I had to come to the place where I could admit the *truth* about what my mother had done, that she had hated me without a cause and abused me physically and emotionally. That was a hard issue to grapple with; how could I believe my mother hates me but that my Heavenly Father loves me? It's an incongruity I wrestled with day and night for years.

Out of the deep pain and dysfunction in my family, my mother abandoned her marriage and her remaining daughter almost two years after I left. This was the catalyst for my father's reconciliation with me, and it gave me an opportunity to return home to seek some of the items I had left behind . . . and to look for answers to my most puzzling questions.

In the cold basement of my parents' home, I found, tucked into a forgotten spare room, the cedar chest containing items from my mother's early marriage years. Buried under crocheted afghans, old birthday cards, wedding mementos, and family photos was my baby book. Beside it was the diary my mother had kept during my preschool years.

I opened Mom's simple journal, a plain office supply pad with the most ordinary blue lines covered in her distinctive, rounded handwriting. It was strange, at first, to hear the mundane accounts of a housewife my own age one generation ago as she bemoaned money problems, housekeeping drudgery, and crying babies just like I did. After a few pages, I nearly forgot whose diary I was reading, I so identified with her frustrations and daily routine.

Until in one day's account the complaints took a darker tone. Without any reason, with no explanation or clue, right after the date, she wrote, "I can't stand Lea Ann. I dread her coming home from preschool every day." And for pages that followed, this distraught mother poured out her emotional anguish at caring for a child she did not want while nursing a baby she adored. And I was that hated child.

I remembered who I was with a start, jerking my head up to see if someone was standing there judging me as I read the forbidden pages. Then I clutched the journal to my chest and ran up two flights of steps to my old bedroom and locked myself in privacy. Curling up on my bed, I pored over the rest of the diary.

The pattern continued. Mom complained about the difficult adjustment to her new life as a stay-at-home mother after her career days. She wished there was more money for vacations and furniture.

She fretted that her husband traveled, but she was anxious for his success. And she adored her new infant daughter who made every day worth living.

She was so conflicted about her relationship with her firstborn that it tainted her diary repeatedly. She confided in the office-ruled pages that she knew her feelings were wrong, but she felt powerless to change her own heart and reframe the relationship. She even wondered, once, if she should seek counseling, but she feared the social stigma of therapy would make things worse. She instead chose to live with the guilt for decades.

The diary ended abruptly when the pages ran out, a dramatic tale with no resolution. But when I looked up with tear-stained cheeks, I knew the end for me. I ripped out every page — every single page — of the notebook and shredded them with my own two hands. Then I threw the fragments into the garbage. Then I emptied the wastebasket into the trash. Then I took out the trash to the garbage canister.

With that, two decades of guilt was gone. The burden of the lie I had lived with for my entire life was released. I knew the truth — *I had done nothing to deserve the abuse.* The truth was there, in Mom's own words. I never had to blame myself again. Even more importantly, I knew that day that *the abuse had nothing to do with me.* My mother was enslaved to her sin, trapped in a darkness she recognized but could not release herself from. Only God could change her heart. Though I believed that my mother was a Christian, I knew then that she had not yet turned to Him for the help she needed to escape the darkness clouding her most intimate relationships. I knew God was pursuing her heart, and I began praying more intentionally that He would bring about the healing she desperately needed.

So now I knew the truth, at long last. I had to own the truth of my story before reconciliation was possible. And I had to wait for my mother to admit the truth before we could meet again. *Reconciliation is only possible through the truth.*

That's why, though the phone rang and the letters flowed from her to me over the months and years that followed, there was little or no response from me other than prayer. I prayed and I waited, trusting God to show me when He would reconcile us by proclaiming the truth from her lips. I knew when she admitted the truth freely that our relationship would be reborn.

That took faith. It felt like, for those ensuing years, that I lived on a different planet and spoke a different language than my mother. I never forgot her, never stopped wondering where she was or what she was doing, never stopped questioning if she thought about me or the grandson she had never met.

Suddenly one evening a couple years later, my husband received a phone call from my mother. I shut myself into my bedroom, unable to bear even hearing his side of the conversation. I only expected more pain, more lies, more abuse. But after nearly an hour, my husband hung up the receiver, came in my room, and sat beside me on the bed. He took my hands in his and said, "I think God is changing your mother's heart, finally, after all this time."

He knew because her first words were apologies. She freely admitted to my husband all the wrong she had done him and asked for his forgiveness. Then she poured out her guilt and sin toward me, sobbing into the phone the years of agony we had lived. Then she asked him, hesitantly, if he believed I could ever talk with her again, if not as daughter to mother, than perhaps as friend to friend.

That night, in detail, David laid out a plan for a renewed relationship with us and gently led both his estranged mother-in-law and his wounded, orphaned wife into a fresh, new love for one another.

Protect Yourself Wisely

Unlike a Hallmark made-for-TV movie, things didn't just bound into perfection while we shared heartfelt moments cutting out cookies and celebrating family holidays. The road to recovery was harder than that for both of us.

We had a lot of catching up to do on our past and present lives. Committed to staying truthful, we both found our first conversations painful, awkward, and scary. There were terse goodbyes when things became too difficult, and there were some misunderstandings and hurt feelings. But we both desperately *wanted* this to work. Mom was eager to prove she was different, and I was desperate for a mother. So we kept at it.

The first several months, our distance was a blessing. We communicated by phone; I was on pregnancy bed rest with nothing but time, and she was recovering from an illness alone, too. We could talk about mundane health concerns, politics, and current events until one of us was brave enough to bring up a memory or question from the past. So we gradually became more comfortable talking about substantial matters while we learned to trust one another anew.

Demonstrate Love

It was not easy. The misunderstandings would spring up out of nowhere. We both had similar, yet contradictory pasts, and we could easily trigger a strong reaction from one another without realizing it. Sometimes we would fight and argue without knowing what we were upset about. Our relationship was confusing, but we were committed to helping one another through it.

One weekend two years later, I flew to my mother's apartment for a visit where we had one of those painful moments. She was curling her hair for church in her bathroom while I put on my makeup at her bedroom mirror. Through the open doors we were talking (I can't remember about what), when suddenly we both found our voices raised and our blood pressure boiling. She stormed through the hall to the family room angrily, while I followed in confusion. When she turned toward me screaming in frustration, I looked deep into her eyes and only saw pain behind my reflection. And my heart broke.

I grabbed my mother's freckled, powerful arms in both my bony hands, not unlike the grasp of the church woman on my own person a few years before. And I earnestly pleaded with Mom to listen to me — not to my words, but to my heart. I reminded her of how far we had come and what miracles God had worked already in both of us. I pleaded with her to not turn back from the path of redemption and grace He had for us. "Mom, I know it is hard for you to understand what *love* is, but you know that God loves you so much. He is the one who put us together, He is the one who ordained our lives would be forever entwined. Because He loves us! And He only wants us to show His love to each other. So, while at times you cannot understand or even believe that I love you, I want you to just hear these words: I will spend the rest of my life demonstrating to you that I love you unconditionally, whether you know it or not."

Neither of us knew how short a time that was. Mom passed away the following year. Her last audible words were, "I love you, Lea Ann."

Live in Faith

I am abundantly blessed. God loves me, He died for me, He saved me from my sin. Christ walked beside me through my painful childhood, revealing Himself to me at a young age and developing my dependence on Him. God allowed me to learn the truth about my pain early in adulthood so that I could give it all fully to Him. And my Heavenly Father miraculously redeemed my relationship with my mother so that we could experience His healing and enjoy a renewed love for one another. Then God gave me the grace to bury my mother, to write her eulogy, and to proclaim His saving work in our lives to our family and friends.

Not all relationships are resolved so neatly here on earth. Most of the time, instead, God allows us to walk on in faith, leaving our misshapen homes and shattered dreams at His feet. Whether you are rebuilding a difficult relationship or struggling to give the burden to your Savior, know this — at the throne of God, it all will be made right. God our Father and judge will bring us together in unity of spirit and love at last, so we all may feast together, complete at last in Him.

What does the Bible say?

Read Psalm 27 and John 17.

What does it mean to you?

Journal your answers and discuss with a friend or your spouse.

1. Are you groping for meaning in an inexplicable pain? Commit to working through the seven steps for healing outlined in the beginning of this chapter. What step are you stumbling on right now?
2. Look carefully at the characteristics of *safe people.* What qualities do you need to work on so you can be a safe person for someone in need?
3. Is there a painful relationship that came to mind while you read this chapter? What steps do you need to take toward healing?
4. How does truth impact painful relationships? How does untruth present barriers to reconciliation? How does bold truth promote healing?
5. How can ordinary wives and mothers and friends initiate healing in the painful relationships around them?
6. When we possess audacious faith that God will reconcile all of His children to one another at last, how does that impact our prayers for one another?

The Great Physician longs to heal our hearts, to restore us to full function.

8

That Painful Past

Shoving myself awkwardly off the doctor's examining table, I shuffled across the sterile room to gaze out the narrow window. Its cold surface against my forehead could not alleviate the burn of tears in my eyes as I gazed at the grey, gloomy winter street below. More excuses, more ambiguity, more meaningless jargon from the rheumatologist behind me healed none of my arthritic pain. More debilitating than my swollen joints, however, was the emotional pain of living apart from my lifelong passion.

"How much longer until I can play the violin again?" I had inquired anxiously at the beginning of the appointment. After over a year of trial-and-error with various drug treatments and physical therapies, I was hungry for hope. I craved just a simple goal, an expectation, some indication that normalcy was around the corner.

"Whoever told you that you would play the violin again?" The doctor's unfeeling response poisoned the room. Stunned silent, I had stumbled across the room to hide the screeching disappointment inflaming my soul.

My entire life, I always wanted to be a violinist. I can vividly recall the first time I heard the instrument at preschool "Show and Tell." Sitting cross-legged on my carpet square, I vowed to myself that one day, I, too, would own this magical instrument and perform even better than my friend Scott did that day. But when I came home to tell my mother my plan, she quickly dismissed my dream; violins were expensive, and teachers were far away.

If my parents wouldn't give me a violin, though, God would. So I took it to the Lord in prayer, just like my Sunday school teachers always told me to. Often and fervently I made the request in child-like faith. I just knew that one day I would indeed become a violinist. In the meantime, I experimented with making violins out of boxes and rubber bands (which did not at all satisfy my craving for a stringed instrument) and listened carefully to the radio whenever I heard a real violinist. When the time came, I would be ready.

So I was overjoyed but not surprised when, five years later, God provided. I not only had real violin lessons, but also a real violin teacher (who even lived in our home for a couple of years!). The private school I attended was beginning a string program, and I was the first student enrolled. Two years later, my beloved instructor introduced me to a master teacher, a professional violinist from the Moscow Philharmonic who had recently defected from the then Soviet Union. I studied with him for over six years. All my dreams came true, and the violin was my particular gift from God. It was difficult, and it was a lot of work, but it was what I had always wanted.

After leaving college early to marry my husband and to start a new life, playing the violin became less of a privilege and more of an obligation. Working low-paying jobs to pay the rent left little time to play, and with no challenging performances on my calendar I had no incentive to practice. Soon my instrument was living in its case, untouched, for months on end, and the sight of it silent in the corner brought waves of guilt. Playing the instrument purchased by my parents brought back painful memories from my childhood, and I began avoiding my first love intentionally.

But if I could hide my violin in the closet, I could not extract it from my soul. The sound of symphonies caused my heart to leap; I would weep at the melody of an orchestra live or over the radio. So I inquired about local philharmonics; surely, if I began performing again, the ghosts of music past would be laid to rest. Alas, now the pull of babies and bills made the regular commitment to rehearsals impossible — until it suddenly wasn't. As year followed year, the financial burden of young adulthood gave way to the stability of middle age. Babies grew into children and teens, and suddenly I found myself with that most rare of commodities — free time. And still the siren song of the violin called. I began dreaming of performing in a local orchestra again, imagining myself among the string section during performances. I even began carrying music scores with me to symphony performances to follow along carefully.

Meanwhile, the occasional pain in my knees had worsened and spread to my ankles and feet, then to my arms and fingers. It took several doctors and countless tests to deliver the news no musician ever wants to hear: inflammatory arthritis.

The pain of arthritis inflamed the regret and guilt I had long suppressed at having laid my violin aside. After a dozen years of joyful praise and a decade of regretful neglect, my precious dream was slipping away. Forever.

And as I began dealing with the Lord about that, I found many more regrets hidden in the back corners of the closet of my heart. As I began pulling out the dirty laundry and hidden trash within my spirit, I discovered a host of broken dreams, torn relationships, misspent hours, hurtful words, neglected commitments. And now, it seemed too late. My time was past, and I had missed it. I had ruined everything.

But after mourning my losses, measuring my guilt, and generally feeling sorry for myself for several weeks, I came to realize that truly, I am not alone. We all are cut from the same cloth, and we all hide the same dirty, filthy rags of sin in our heart closets. That's why Christ had to come, to sacrifice His blood to clothe us in new garments. So like the Psalmist, I finally understood what that new song was he played, the praise to God who found him ruined in the quicksand of sin to lift him up and set his feet on the rock (Psalm 40). I had to recognize the horrible dirt of my sin to appreciate the gift of my salvation each day.

At last I knew the answer to my doctor's question. Who had told me I could ever play the violin again? *The God who gave me that violin in the first place.* He would put a new song in my heart and on my hands in His own time. But first, I had to deal with that painful past.

Do you, too, struggle with a painful, inflamed spirit? Is your soul sick with the sin of past mistakes? Are you hiding the laundry of regret in the closet of your heart, flinging discarded dreams over the pile in an attempt to hide it, to forget the passion and purpose you once knew?

The Great Physician longs to heal our hearts, to restore us to full function. Who told you that your heart would ever sing again? *Your Heavenly Father did.* Here's His prescription for health.

Choose the Right Doctors

That rheumatologist, with his dire predictions and Band-Aid® approach to my illness, was no real help. And his disinterest in returning me to full function was discouraging, to say the least. When I gathered my purse and my young son from the exam room to limp out into the hall, my seven-year-old turned around and asked, "Why are you a doctor, anyway, if you don't like curing people?" The shocked doctor just stared as I fumbled for my boy's hand and hurried him away.

But the little boy was right, I realized later. Why was I continuing to visit a doctor who was not helping me? I returned to my general practitioner for advice, and he took over managing my health himself. And you know what? With his wise advice and careful guidance, I steadily improved from that point on.

The Lord is the Great Physician not only of our bodies, but also of our souls. He has provided local doctors: pastors and counselors who apply the Word of truth to our hearts and lives so we can grow complete, prepared for God's work (2 Timothy 3:16). For our own spiritual health, it is vitally important we regularly visit — and participate in — a Bible believing, Bible preaching church. There is no substitute.

Find a Trustworthy Physical Therapist

I had to practice several months of physical therapy to regain function in my hands and strength in my legs and arms. And I hated every minute of it. Exercise is the curse.

But my physical therapist was kind, sympathetic, sensitive, and wise. He empathized with the pain I felt, and he took steps every visit to make me as comfortable as possible. He anticipated the setbacks common in my illness, so he knew when to push me further in the exercises and when to let me rest. And he never stopped encouraging me that one day I would be just as strong as ever.

We all need friends like that, safe people like those we talked about in the last chapter. We need friends who love us, care for us, and help us be our best no matter what challenges we face. Not everyone can handle the intimate details of our recovery, so we need to be discerning who we entrust with our healing journey. True friends will listen to our fears without judging, pray for our healing without criticism, tell us the truth with love, and push us onward with patience. These friends are essential companions on the road to recovery.

Take the Right Medicine Regularly

I tried several different drug treatments in the early months of my arthritis diagnosis. Some were mildly helpful; others didn't do anything for me at all. One drug, though, seemed to effect a tremendous improvement until I had a terrifying reaction: sudden, deep depression and unrelenting suicidal thoughts. The wrong medicine, I found, is much worse than no medicine.

This is so true when we are dealing with our painful past. Bookstores, media, and even popular Christianity are full of the *wrong answers* to our painful past, our besetting sin, our personal failures and losses. We cannot pull ourselves up. We cannot heal ourselves. We can't cure our pain, paint over it, diet it, exercise it, or envision it into oblivion. God didn't make the world to work that way, and when we put our trust in *man's solution* to our spiritual problem, we will end up oh, so much worse.

Healing from our painful past and deliverance from sin habits only comes through the regular application of God's Word. We must regularly reapply God's solutions by studying the Scriptures, memorizing the verses, and meditating on the truths of God that counter the lies of Satan and the world around us.

This is the daily, faith-filled activity that most restores our soul-health and strengthens the muscles of our heart. All of us, no matter how we live or where we serve or what position we hold, fight the inflammation of sin disease within our beings. God's curing regimen is free, but His words must be habitually consumed throughout the day for maximum effectiveness.

Eat a Healthy Diet

One surprising finding among my many medical tests to determine the cause of my disease was my severe vitamin deficiency. Well, maybe the deficiency itself wasn't a surprise, but my inability to raise my vitamins levels after months of healthy eating and mega-doses of vitamins puzzled doctors. In fact, I was still going the wrong direction; my early-onset osteopenia (thinning of the bones) worsened after two years of heavy vitamin therapy.

It appeared, after all, that something was keeping me from absorbing the nutrients my body desperately needed, and nearly every system in my body was beginning to show symptoms of malnutrition: my skin broke out in sores, my hair fell out in handfuls, my nails peeled apart, my digestive system soured, and my energy plummeted. We soon found the reason — some things I was eating, foods that were healthy for most people, were actually harmful to my systems. So as a result, the healthy food and nutrients I was eating were not being processed effectively. The food that was bad for me obstructed all the healthy nutrition.

It was an easy problem to fix, though. Once we identified my harmful foods (gluten and dairy), I could eat everything else and feel much better. The difference was remarkable. Within a few weeks, I felt like a new woman and my blood tests showed a clear improvement.

Sometimes when we are struggling to recover from a painful past or to overcome a sin issue, we are discouraged that no progress is coming. We take our medicine and do our therapy and consume God's Word regularly, but our souls remain sick. We need to take a closer look then at what else our heart is consuming. Something we enjoy may actually be unhealthy for us.

We must remove those items, habits, and relationships that are harmful for our sprititual health. This is not legalism, and it's not a one-rule-fits-all mandate. We each know what our strengths and weaknesses are and where our sensitivities lie. An important part of healing is avoiding triggers by avoiding activities, people, media, and situations that increase the activity of our disease or further inflame our fleshly passions.

It isn't always easy, either. We crave what our flesh wants, and that craving brings greater bondage to the trigger issue. In my case, I loved all things doughy and cheesy — exactly what had to be discarded. I missed pizza and cheeseburgers and lasagna so much at first. The struggle was real. But the longer I disciplined my eating habits, replacing what was wrong for me with what was good for me, the more my health strengthened. After a few weeks, I felt so wonderful that I didn't even desire the trigger foods anymore. You can eat lasagna and cheese bread right in front of me, and I won't drool at all. I look at the plate and only see *pain,* and I don't want any part of that.

That is true recovery — a change of mind about both our sin *and* what leads to the sin. When we identify what leads us away from spiritual health, away from the joy of God's best for us, away from the intimacy of Him, we simply must replace that issue with God alone. And after a time of feasting wholeheartedly on only what God designed for our good, we will lose appetite for the enslaving sin of this world.

That's why this change of appetite is the opposite of legalism. I can't eat wholewheat bread and Greek yogurt, but I know that both may be just what the doctor ordered for you. My particular triggers aren't yours, and your specialized healthy diet isn't mine. When we both recognize that and encourage one another to follow the healthy plan God set for each of us, we find so much freedom and acceptance.

Stay Active

It comes as no surprise that a major part of my recovery was *exercise.* In spite of my swollen joints and painful limbs, I had to keep moving every day. The more I lay in bed, the worse I became. But when I regularly walked and biked and jogged, I began seeing my overall function return and my pain diminish.

It wasn't easy, though. I had to lower my expectations and simply be content with just moving a little some days, and I had to readjust my perspective with my slow, uneven progress. If I just got out of bed each morning, cared for my children, and walked around a little, I improved steadily.

That's why my pastor's advice for discouragement is so helpful. When depressed or disabled spiritually or emotionally, he has a simple formula for survival: "Do the next thing." Make the bed. Wash the laundry. Cook the meal. Bathe the child. Show up to work and get the job done. It's a simple and effective remedy.

We don't have the answer to every problem right now, and we won't find an instantaneous cure for our painful past. But we do know what we are supposed to do *right now,* those mundane chores that take little thought and all the effort in our feeble bodies. Do it. Do it right now, and leave the rest to the Great Physician.

After a couple years practicing *the next thing,* I knew it was time for the next big step. I got my violin out of its dusty case and began practicing regularly. My stiff fingers rebelled at first, but slowly the skill and training began to return. I began playing in church occasionally, and then I scheduled that orchestra audition. And nailed it.

The truth is that *I wasn't going to regain the ability to play the violin until I began regularly playing the violin.* So sure, I made a fool out of myself for more than one rehearsal. My tone was strident and my fingers far too slow. But each week I practiced harder, and each performance I heard clear improvement.

And my love was back.

Get back into the ministry God called you to. You know what it is — the passion He placed within your soul, the creative mark of divinity He implanted in your life. Bravely follow His calling for you, even before you are perfectly polished. Because the fact of the matter is that you won't be perfect. Ever. You will be healed, you will be healthy, and you will be used of God mightily right where you are.

You just need to show up and start making the music.

What does the Bible say?

Read Psalm 39–40 and Ephesians 1.

What does it mean to you?

Journal your answers and discuss with a friend or your spouse.

1. What gift or dream have you been guiltily shoving into the back of your heart's closet?
2. Which habit for recovery do you need to work on? How will you practice it this week?
3. How can you take these habits and help someone else?
4. How is your spiritual diet? What entertainment or activities do you need to eliminate? What will you replace them with?
5. How active are you in your home, in your community, and in your church? How can you better exercise your unique gifts and abilities this month?
6. Do you have an exercise partner, a friend to partner with you for better spiritual health? Agree together to pray for one another, encourage each other, and hold each other accountable.

We are God's special creation, the very image of His person on earth.

9

Painful People

"Who do you think you are?" the man stepped forward menacingly. Clutching my pile of music to my chest, I stumbled backward into the cold concrete wall of the church basement. I glanced around the dimly lit hallway, praying someone would come around the corner to rescue me, but all I could see was the looming figure hulking over me.

"Why don't you go back to wherever it was you came from?" He leaned forward until his face was inches from mine. "We don't need you here."

"I can't." The sobs choked my throat and clouded my brain. I felt slow, stupid, confused. Helpless. "We moved here to serve," I protested weakly. "I'm just here to help you, that's all." *Where is everyone? Why can't we keep the lights turned on in this basement hallway?*

"Well, you are *no help at all!* I wish you had never come here!" He swung around on his heels and stomped up the stairs. "Now, get up here and start playing the piano for rehearsal. YOU'RE LATE!"

The irony of his demand wasn't lost on me, but I remained frozen to the wall in terror. I hastily wiped my sleeve across my face, ran fingers over my hair, and took a deep breath. In a moment, I could hear his steps cross the church auditorium over my head, and I knew it was safe to enter the stairwell. Just a few steps up and through the heavy swinging door, then I was in the sanctuary — a place of refuge that felt anything but safe. Avoiding eye contact with the choir, I slipped onto the piano bench and began to play the accompaniment for next Sunday's worship number. Over the lid of the grand piano, I watched the choir director laugh and joke with his eager followers, his periodic glances over his shoulder toward me the only indication of his alter ego.

What Can I Do?

I worried. I was certain no one would believe me if I tried to speak up. The choir director was probably the most popular man in the church; everyone admired his dedication and humor. The person I most needed to tell (and should have told immediately) was my husband, but I feared the fallout. Since we had moved across the country to join this ministry, we had constantly struggled to make ends meet and to make friends. The stress was taking a toll on my husband, and this could be the last straw. I felt so alone, so isolated, so confused. I decided to just shut up and put up with it.

When you first meet a bully, you probably won't recognize him. Your bully could be a coworker, a family member, a church member, or even a close friend, so even if you suspect you are encountering a bully, you may be tempted to dismiss or excuse the behavior. You'll blame circumstances (the economy, a tragedy, an illness) or a bad mood or a misunderstanding. Then when the bullying continues or even escalates, you may blame yourself — if only you had performed better or worked harder or said the right thing or made the right gesture, maybe it all could have been avoided.

Until you begin to wonder: could you be the victim of bullying?

When we think of bullying, we tend to imagine playground children picking on one another or a gang of boys beating up a weaker child for his lunch money. But chances are you or someone you know is being harassed by an adult bully.

I don't use that term lightly, and it is important to understand what does and does not indicate bullying. Like other hot-topic words like *harassment* and *abuse*, misuse of the word can backfire, leading to desensitivity and inaction on behalf of legitimate problems. In other words, let's not be the little girls who cried *BULLY* at every cross look.

Just as importantly, though, *when it comes to bullying, it is imperative we call it what it is.* Sweeping the behavior under the rug, excusing abuse of power, blaming victims, and denying the facts only perpetuates the cycle of abuse, enables bullies to continue, and injures everyone involved. Instead, we want to be part of the cure. Identifying the problem is the first step to safety and recovery in our lives and in the lives of women to whom we minister.

What Is Bullying, Then?

Bullying is the aggressive, intentional, repeated act of intimidation. The bully seeks to render the victim powerless, humiliated, and controlled through fear, stress, and/or physical harm.

It is easy to confuse bullying with other mean-spirited behavior, so this is how I distinguish the common labels. *Abuse* is a deviant departure from societal norms to harm someone sexually, physically, or emotionally; most abuse is defined legally or institutionally. *Harassment* crosses a personal boundary after the victim or institution (like a workplace code of conduct) has indicated a moral boundary. Most harassment is also defined by organizations, and habitual harassment turns into an abusive situation. In contrast to abuse or harrassment, *bullying* attempts to undermine a victim's sense of self and security while staying within societal and institutional norms. So, while a bully clearly has intent to harm, he carefully works within the legal limits in order to further prevent the victim's obtaining help. The music director was technically not doing anything illegal when he stepped into my personal space and chastised me, but he had no intention of being a blessing to me; he wanted to intimidate (and even eliminate) me while remaining blameless.

As women active in our churches and communities, we will meet bullies. We will witness friends being bullied, and we will likely be bullied ourselves. I have met a bully in nearly every ministry and workplace in which I have been associated. You can likely think of adult bullies you have encountered, too. Maybe you are being bullied right now.

Please remember that *you did nothing to cause this trial.* You didn't ask to be persecuted. When you are habitually exposed to bullying, though, the confusion grows. You may begin questioning every action you take, every word you say, and even your current lifestyle. In time, escaping the pain of bullying can cloud your judgment, as every part of you seems to scream, "Just make it stop!" By better understanding the sin of bullying, we can better protect ourselves, and we can better minister to those hurting around us.

Bullying Is Sin

It is unbiblical, un-Christian, immoral, inappropriate behavior. In both spirit and in action, bullying goes against any reasonable behavior expected in the community, workplace, school, or society. Its very essence is unloving and uncharitable.

For example, a bully at work may require an employee to repeatedly perform the same menial, tedious tasks (typically outside her job description) while berating her publicly or privately. In one ministry, a bully at church interrupted a class to demand the pregnant teacher mop up sewage in the restroom "to display a servant's heart" during regular class time. A cyber bully hacked into the victim's personal social media account and then informed the victim that she had done so to intimidate and silence her.

Bullying Has a Clear Purpose to Harm

Oftentimes, the bully will state outright his motivation to the victim or to others. The goal is usually to eliminate the victim (get her fired, remove her as competition, minimize her contribution) and cause irreparable harm physically, emotionally, or financially. In that music ministry, the leader told me that he wanted me to leave the church. In another case, I had a boss tell me that her goal was to make sure I had no more friends and never held another job. You may see a bully ministry leader use private counseling sessions as public examples with thinly veiled identifying details to intimidate the victim (and those hearing it) into silence and compliance. A cyber bully may leak humiliating information or use confidential information to blackmail and intimidate the victim.

Bullying Causes Genuine Loss

The bully damages the victim's reputation, confidence, and performance. The victim is left confused and injured, losing her confidence and strength. She likely questions her own perception of reality, her ability to make sound judgments, and her own personal worth. She becomes increasingly doubtful of her ability to do her job, to maintain her personal privacy and security, and even her ability to use her natural talents and abilities effectively. If those around her choose to believe the bully rather than reach out to the victim, she no longer has help when she needs it most.

Sometimes we aren't sure if we are dealing with a difficult friend, an overbearing leader, or a true bully. Here are some questions to ask yourself to determine if you are being bullied.

- Is this an accumulation of incidents or a regular *pattern* of behavior?
- Is this treatment *unwarranted* (you did nothing to cause it) or disproportionate to their stated reason for harming you?
- Is this person *ungrateful* for the work or ministry you do for her or for the organization?
- Is this person driven by *jealousy*?
- Is this person someone you have a *relationship* with (friend, coworker, church member)?
- Does this person have an attitude of *fault-finding* in an undermining manner, rather than coaching for your success?
- Does this person *twist* your words and actions to others, even gossiping or slandering?
- Does this person frequently *rearrange* relationships to further her goals and hide her abusive patterns (changing churches, cutting off friends, firing employees)?
- Does the bully attempt to *isolate* you from family members, friends, or coworkers who should be supporting you?
- Does this person *intimidate* you with statements like, "It's just your word against mine" or "No one will believe you"?

If you just said *yes* to most of those questions, you are dealing with a bully. You may feel shocked or in disbelief, perhaps because the bully does not appear like you once imagined. But bullies can be women or men, family members or neighbors, close friends or church leaders.

A few years ago, a close friend turned against me. I thought she loved me as dearly as I loved her, but suddenly she began sending me vile messages filled with hateful accusations and sickening language. She publicly accused me to others and refused to talk with me personally about the disagreement. She would only email or text, and then only demands and orders. She twisted my words in slander, and she lied about my other friends to my face, saying everyone hated me and had told her so. Then she hacked into my social media accounts and blog in an attempt to intimidate me.

The confusion I felt at first turned to horror, then fear, then intimidation. The obscene and threatening messages came several times a day, sometimes flooding my inbox all at once with dozens of emails. Soon I was afraid to open my own computer or answer my phone. The stress became so great that the sound of my mobile notifications triggered a physical, nauseating response. I lost 15 pounds in two weeks from the stress.

Finally, one evening I sat up in bed all of a sudden, turned to my husband, and asked, "Am I being bullied?"

And without hesitation, he said, "Yes, of course you are." I was shocked, because it had not crossed my mind that my close friend, the woman I had loved and prayed for and helped nearly every single day for years, could be a *bully.* Could a Christian friend, someone I thought I was serving the Lord alongside, become my enemy?

Bullying Is the Opposite of Christ-like Love

God loves and values you and me, and we Christians should always love one another. It is our love for one another that shows all the world that we follow Jesus. When we are being bullied, the first thing we need to remember is that *this person is not modeling Christ.* This behavior is not God's working; it is of our enemy.

It is imperative that we protect ourselves from bullying. As long as bullying continues, the work of God is being opposed. God's plan for me and for you is entirely too important to allow the enemy to intimidate, threaten, or persecute it away from us. For our safety and for the work of Christ, we must not tolerate bullying.

That's why that night, I didn't sleep until I had made a plan with my husband on how we would deal with my bully. And over the next few days, as the behavior escalated, we continually modified the plan until I was safe from her influence. I forwarded all the threatening emails to my husband, who kept them for legal records. I then blocked her email address and phone number so I would no longer receive the harassing messages. I regained control of my online presence and constructed safeguards so outsiders could not gain access. I then changed everything that triggered that fearful, emotional response: a new look on my computer, new ringtones for mobile notifications, and even a new daily routine. Meanwhile, my husband sought legal counsel to ensure our family's safety in spite of continued threats.

My recovery from that bullying took months, though. I had been left confused, disoriented, and afraid. I had lost my confidence, my perspective, and my dear friend whom I sincerely loved, as well as several other friends who chose to believe her lies. So it took several months to restore my confidence and to heal from the pain.

But I did heal after I slowly worked through that same healing process I had learned many years before. I had to *accept the truth* that the woman I thought was my friend had set herself as my enemy; she didn't love me. I had to bravely *admit the truth* that we weren't friends, even if it cost me other relationships. I found *safe friends* like my husband, my best friend, and my pastor, and I confided my trial to each of them so they could pray for me and counsel me through recovery. I *re-examined my beliefs* about friendships and my personal boundaries so I could better protect myself in the future. Then I allowed myself plenty of *time* to rest in the Lord and to allow Him to heal my heart.

It is not likely that we will be reconciled to our bullies here on earth. By its very nature, bullying directly opposes God's work in our lives. We simply must trust our Heavenly Father to settle the score and to set everything right in His perfect timing. The cure for bullying in our families and in our churches remains clear: we can protect God's work within our community by following that same plan for restoring relationships.

1. Know God's plan. God's will for all of us is to glorify Himself. He created us to enjoy intimate fellowship with Him now and forever. When we keep our relationship with Christ foremost in our daily activities and personal relationships, there is no room for the mean-spirited nature of harassment to continue. When continued bullying interferes with our joyful fellowship with our Heavenly Father, we must recognize the problem and take steps to return to the center of His will.

2. Set healthy boundaries. We must remember our position as God's special creation, the very image of His person on earth. As His children, we must treat that relationship with God with respect and honor. Just as I would not tolerate someone defaming or desecrating my church or my pastor, I should not allow anyone to profane the person God created me to be. We cannot hesitate to defend God's plan in our lives, His image in our personality. Remembering God's purpose in our lives clarifies those healthy boundaries with others.

3. Exalt the truth. The sin of bullying is dependent on lies, slander, and innuendo. When we shine the light of truth in our conversation and conduct, there is little place for the evil to hide. Boldly tell the truth — and only the truth — to the safe people in your life. Don't hesitate to correct the lies bullies speak in your presence. Consistent honesty powerfully defends your reputation from long-term harassment, because bullies cannot blow the smoke of falsehood forever.

4. Protect yourself. We simply must honor God's will in our lives and homes and churches by guarding against distractions. Small things, like not answering the phone after 9 p.m. or not checking email before devotions or not responding to criticism until a day later . . . these little guidelines can protect our minds and hearts and emotions and energies so that we can properly care for our God-given responsibilities. Furthermore, by setting these protections in our lives, we can help ourselves not fall into the trap of sin or harming someone else.

5. Demonstrate love. Bullying is the opposite of love, and bullying cannot exist with love. Our Christianity, our churches, and our families must be characterized by this true affection for one another:

- Unifying, not isolating
- Encouraging, not belittling
- Edifying, not destructive
- Serving, not domineering
- Peaceful, not argumentative
- Healing, not persecuting
- Inclusion, not pre-judging
- Sincerity, not pretension
- Honesty, not deception
- Admission, not manipulation
- Consistency, not fluctuation
- Giving, not jealous

> These six things the LORD hates,
> Yes, seven are an abomination to Him:
> A proud look,
> A lying tongue,
> Hands that shed innocent blood,
> A heart that devises wicked plans,
> Feet that are swift in running to evil,
> A false witness who speaks lies,
> And one who sows discord among brethren (Proverbs 6:16–19).

Dear friend, God loves you and hates the sin of bullying. If you find yourself in such a relationship, please reach out for help and take steps today to protect yourself. I'm praying for your recovery.

What does the Bible say?

Read Psalm 41 and Psalm 55.

What does it mean to you?

Journal your answers and discuss with a friend or your spouse.

1. Outline the progress of emotions from the beginning to end in these two Psalms. What does David say happened to him? How does he feel about the betrayals?

2. What verse number indicates a change in David's attitude? What causes his heart to change?
3. What specific requests does David make, and what does he specifically praise God for doing?
4. Do you have a bully in your life now, or did you in the recent past? What steps do you need to take toward healing and protection?
5. What clues could you watch for to identify bullying actions in your home, ministry, or community? How can you be the healing solution?

Significant Influence

Part IV

We must serve God every day, right where we are.

10

Leading from the Pew

Christian women often picture *church leadership* as men in suits. We imagine our pastors, elders, deacons, and teachers who are up front waving their arms and their Bibles, handing out bulletins and doctrinal statements, managing the money and the building projects, and generally keeping everyone holy and in their assigned pews as always being males. This is the cultural stereotype that we grew up with, a male-dominated church leadership model. And everywhere today this stereotype is under attack. Major denominations are installing women pastors. Television networks air women speaking to audiences of thousands. Both liberal and conservative Christians are wrestling with the question of what roles a woman can or cannot fill within a biblical church structure.

And we're asking all the wrong questions.

Instead of splitting hairs over whether Paul did or did not consider women when he wrote letters to Timothy outlining church structure; instead of arguing about what church roles are meant by *elder* and *deacon*; instead of debating what qualifications are symbolic and which are literal; instead of making a theological issue out of gender in the church, let's ask the real question:

Are we women intentionally using our gifts and talents within our local church to maximize our service for God?

Because if we believe that God created each of us in His image, if we believe that He endowed each of us with unique God-like talents and abilities, if we believe that God's plan for His church includes each member of the body working together for the health and productivity of the whole, if we believe our theology drives our actions and attitudes each day, if we really believe God's Word is relevant for our lives today, then we simply must stop sitting on the sidelines and lounging in the pews. We have to stand up and get active. Ladies, we cannot wait for someone to give us a role or a title or a committee or an ordination — *we must serve God every day, right where we are.*

God created us. God made us in His own image. God granted us individual, customized talents and abilities. Before the foundation of the world He planned for each one of us and how He would use our lives and relationships and activities for His glory. God needs us to fulfill His plan by glorifying Him while ministering in our local churches.

Throughout the New Testament we see women leading within the Early Church. And surprisingly, none of them asked for permission or waited for an official title — they just met the needs around them.

- Mary and her friends joined the disciples in the upper room to pray for the filling of the Spirit (Acts 1:14).
- The Apostle Phillip's four daughters prophesied publicly (Acts 21:9).
- Priscilla wasn't shy about training Apollos in Bible doctrine (Acts 18:26).
- Phoebe financially supported and served as a deacon at the church in Kechries, a port village for Corinth (Romans 16:1–2).
- Euodia and Syntyche were strong apologists for the faith, even to the point of becoming argumentative (Philippians 4:2–3).

The Book of Acts and Paul's epistles describe women serving right alongside men, church members coming together regardless of gender or background and laying aside their differences to exalt the gospel. This was always God's plan — complete unity in Christ (Galatians 3:23–29).

We women have tremendous influence within our local church — opportunities to further the gospel, to minister to the hurting, to draw the body together, and to lift up the name of Christ. The work of God is not confined to a select few, is it? We are all commanded to serve one another, to reach the lost, and to glorify God. We must renew our prayer each day to "start the work with me." God wants to use us, and He expects us to be leading within the church right from our pews.

I am reminded again of the young mother who juggles feeding schedules and diaper changes to participate in our choir ministry each Sunday. No matter how sleep-deprived or stressed, she greets nursery workers every week with a wide smile and a sincere offer to help, just as comfortable on the floor with whiny, sticky toddlers as on the platform with a shiny, new songbook. Hardly a week goes by that she doesn't text me a verse of Scripture or ask how she can pray for me. Her faithfulness, sincerity, and joy in Christ in the midst of the daily trials all mothers face are a constant encouragement to me.

Several years ago, one of the godliest women I ever knew literally gave me the coat off her back. Mrs. Schmidt was an immigrant who proudly raised several children and apparently memorized the entire Bible. At least, that's what the congregation believed, because not an opportunity passed her by without her quoting something for everyone's edification in her thick accent and confident voice. No one at church could mention a prayer request or ask for testimonies or talk about spiritual things at all in her presence unless we were prepared for entire chapters of the Bible to be quoted loudly, with feeling and personal commentary. Yet there was not an ounce of hypocrisy within her witness, just bright-eyed, clear-voiced evidence of a lifetime walked close beside her Heavenly Father.

Throughout a particularly brutal winter, Mrs. Schmidt observed my struggle through ministry challenges, public criticism, sick children, and even my husband's surgery. At least once a month, she scrawled a verse of Scripture on a piece of paper and pressed it into my hand with a whispered, "God sees you, and I'm praying for you." And so when I trudged up the aisle one week after services, ready to quit because the burden of family and ministry had become too heavy, I was startled when her frail arms pulled me aside and thrust her fur coat upon me. "Wear this. The coat is heavy for me, and I know life is heavy for you. Oh, you didn't have to say a thing — God showed me when I was praying for you this week. And, like I said, I can't wear this coat anymore. I'm not strong enough. You are. You are strong enough. God gave it to you to wear. And you will wear it beautifully, just like He beautifully enables you to do the work He has for you." And with a pat on my arm, she shuffled away.

God enables each of us to beautifully wear the coat of ministry right where we are. Sometimes, though, it does feel heavy (and maybe too scratchy or too warm). That doesn't mean we should lay it aside, because even if we don't recognize it at first, our ministry cloak is tailor-made for each of us. Our Creator fashioned a mantle of loveliness to adorn our work for Him with modesty, beauty, and power. God's plan is always for us to put on our ministry cloak every day, to use the distinct abilities and opportunities He designed for us, leading others to Him right from our pew.

Family in the Ministry

Leading from the pew starts at home. Our work for God is either magnified or hindered by our relationships within our own four walls. You know it's true. How many ministries have we seen falter because of a marital breakup or a rebellious child?

This has obvious implications for my friends who are married to their pastor (bless your hearts), those who lead a mission organization, and those who are serving in a public speaking ministry. But the rest of us pew-warmers are not exempt from this qualification. *If we profess Christ, we must first demonstrate our faith and love at home.*

In my early years of ministry, I failed here miserably. My face is all shades of scarlet when I remember the long hours of service at church while my family at home needed me more: my husband pleading with me to spend romantic time but I was too tired from long rehearsals for special services; my children whining, hungry, and bored while I scolded them for not sitting quietly and waiting out rehearsals in the sanctuary; my own house dusty and unkempt while I volunteered for church cleanup and organization weekends.

There are seasons of sacrifice (VBS, anyone?), there are periods of pushing through for a special emphasis (hello, revival meetings), there are times to roll up our sleeves and get the work done for the furtherance of the ministry. *But when 150 percent commitment to church work overtakes the housework and personal relationships, we are sacrificing what is sacred for a profane purpose.*

That is the most important lesson every woman in ministry must learn first and often, no matter what our role may be. Our most significant contribution to the Kingdom, outside of our own love for God Himself, will be our active love for our husband and children, our enabling of their ministry through our consistent care for them.

Our care for each family member's physical, emotional, and spiritual needs empowers each of them to then turn around and give to others. We often don't recognize how important this is. We meet our husband's physical needs, giving him love and care and affection so he can confidently walk out the door each Sunday satisfied, healthy, and refreshed — ready to think of others and reach out to them. We fill hungry bellies before Sunday school and pack nursery snacks and hide candy in our purses so growling tummies don't distract from God's lessons for little ones. We dress them, smooth down their hair, and tie their church shoes so they can skip into service at their best, ready to reflect God's beauty in their radiant little faces. We get up extra early on everyone else's day of rest to make sure our household is prepared to worship and minister.

We teach our young people that God's house is sacred by training them to sit still, walk slowly, and speak softly in church. We emphasize to our teens that ministry is a responsibility by waking them up early, driving them regularly, and reminding them of their commitments. We demonstrate to our husband that we are unified in the Body of Christ by picking up the slack in his chosen ministry.

Day in and day out, we make the adjustments and juggle the schedules to make sure everyone arrives on time for special meetings, we cook crockpot meals and drill verses to help each child prepare for Bible club, we run carpools, take turns in the nursery, fill in for Sunday school teachers, bake cookies, and cut out flannel graphs for family members to share God's truth with others. In a hundred little ways we facilitate the work our spouse and children do for Christ each week. These actions, more than our words, show our loved ones what it means to represent the image of God at church.

So while I am fond of saying that women do lead from the church pew, we must first lead *within* the church pew. God never intended for us to sacrifice our spouse and our children on the altar of service. Indeed, *God gave us that husband and those children before the church,* and it is our primary responsibility to care for their needs.

Almost two decades ago, I bashfully confided my marital frustrations as a young bride to my pastor's wife. My husband was not doing things the way I wanted him to, and neither of us were satisfied with our marriage. The pastor's wife listened patiently as I listed my grievances, then she wisely told me, "Well, I hope you get things right with your husband before Sunday. You can't come serve God unless you first are reconciled with him." She pointed out Matthew 5:24 to me, and I shame-facedly went home to apologize to David. She was right — my sacrificial love for my husband was far more important than winning any private battle with him or performing any act of public service.

Sadly, that same woman who taught me this important truth was unable to follow it herself, and a decade later her ministry ended in divorce. In the aftermath, not only her husband and children, but an entire church was severely wounded — all because of the breakdown in this one relationship. I am convinced that we cannot make a lasting contribution for God if we ignore our sacred responsibility to love our husband unconditionally. We must keep first things first.

Ironically, serving God at home cures much of our stress in the ministry. I have found that when I keep my priorities in check — my personal relationship with God, then my relationship with each of my family members — that serving others becomes less of a burden. I have the freedom, the resources, and the emotional and spiritual energy to reach out to others. Conversely, when I am pushing my husband aside and dragging my children behind me just to get more done at church, ministry becomes a heavy burden, another chore on the endless to-do list.

When we have cared for our family and provided for their physical, emotional, and spiritual needs, we can then help our fellow church members. Our New Testament sisters remind us that we can't become nearsighted in our ministry. It's not just my pew that counts; I need to look across the aisle at the woman who needs me to reach out and make a difference for her.

I easily become so absorbed in the mundane housekeeping, the enormous responsibility of rearing and teaching children, taking care of my husband, meeting the demands of a busy family that I sink into my seat each Sunday exhausted and needy. "God, just give me something to keep me going," is my most-often prayer during the moment of silent meditation (and my daughter thinks I am praying for more ideas on how to make her life difficult). I just need grace. Grace and mercy. "More, please" is about all I can squeeze out of my soul by mid-morning Sunday.

And I forget that the woman sitting right behind me just breathed that same prayer, too.

My church isn't there just to meet my needs and fill my cup and disciple my family. God made me a member of that body of believers so I would fulfill a ministry to my brothers and sisters in Christ. I can't become so focused on my own wants that I neglect those around me.

We women know what helps most in times of difficulty — and isn't nearly every week a time of difficulty for a young mother or frazzled homeschooler or harried single parent or exhausted working mom? That word of encouragement, that hug of friendship, that whispered prayer mean the world to a weary soul. And when we bring a helpful devotional to borrow or a new journal to fill with prayers or a pound of coffee to fuel another week of service, we give our sisters in Christ a hand up on the road of life. We must never underestimate the power of the ministry of encouragement, for we know that we ourselves depend on it.

No matter how big or small our local church, no matter how new our family or established our membership, no matter the size of our role or sphere of influence, we always find some people easier to encourage than others. It's the truth. We have our best Sunday school buddy, the helpful lady who brings the good potlucks, the entertaining teacher, the fun activities coordinator, and the grandmotherly prayer warrior. And then, there's that woman across the aisle that just rubs us the wrong way.

God wants us to reach her. She needs our ministry.

The rest of the world is all about popularity and celebrity, good looks and abilities, friend numbers and best-dressed lists, but not God's Church. In God's economy, it's the less popular, more needy, least-likely-to-help-me-ever that most deserves love, affection, prayer, and support. That's true, faith-defining love.

We know that. We teach our children that. And it hurts us when we don't make it into the "in group" at church, when we aren't chosen for the popular small group or asked to lead the ministry. We hate to be the ones on the outside, but our human nature isn't naturally inclusive, either. We must constantly fight *against* this divisive spirit of cliques to preserve the unity of our congregation. Every time we reach out, we strengthen God's ministry.

Our faithfulness, too, is a powerful force for good within our church. Why does 1 Corinthians 4:2 list *faithfulness* as the sole qualification for service, if not because *showing up makes all the difference.* God doesn't call us to be brilliantly talented or immensely influential; He calls us to just be faithful. Just keep going, just keep attending, just keep doing what is right each day, each week.

Knowing Where You're Called — No Matter What

At your church, don't you know who is faithful? There are always one or two women in every congregation who are always there, always ready, always prepared to help others. She's the one you call for help in the nursery at the last minute; she's always front and center in the choir. She never complains about teaching preschool VBS or hosting missionaries or filling in at the last minute. You know she will be there next week. You want to be like her when you grow up.

I know just such a young woman, a young lady who has set an example for many of us twice her age. For years, she faithfully put the needs of one handicapped teen ahead of her own, ministering not only during the services, but even throughout the week to show God's love and care. Every week, year after year, she stayed beside her disabled friend to help her navigate the high-energy children's programs at church. She patiently drilled Scripture verses and doctrinal truths until they were clearly understood, helping her classmate achieve awards for Bible knowledge she herself would never receive. She saw a need, and she humbly and faithfully met that need.

God placed that remarkable lady within the body of this local church for that exact purpose at that exact time. And when she exercised her spiritual gifts faithfully, God used her in a mighty way not only in that one life she poured herself into, but in the lives of all of us who beheld it.

This is what Paul is talking about in Ephesians chapter 4. The different gifts and abilities He has placed within our local congregation fit together to complete the entire body and to glorify the Creator of us all. We don't want to see the body disjointed, but that's exactly what happens when we do not serve in the areas God intended us to. Sometimes that means we have to step out of our pew and reach across the aisle. At other times, it may require us to walk up front in active leadership.

We don't always want to exercise the gifts and callings God has given us. Sometimes that ministry coat does feel heavy, itchy, and hot. Ministry means *meeting the needs of people,* and that adds to the weight of our duties. Some of the people God has called us to serve feel irritating or prickly, and it takes a lot of effort not to scratch back, and sometimes the criticism and scrutiny just make us sweat. Yet the faithful women who pass us this cloak of ministry urge us to put it on and to wear it beautifully.

Public criticism is especially painful, no matter what your role in the church. In my mid-twenties, I experienced this as church music director in a conservative East Coast church. Many of the men had very definite ideas of what a woman's role in the church should be: in the nursery or in the kitchen. So when the senior pastor asked me to conduct the church orchestra, several protested loudly. One publicly walked out of rehearsal and left the church after letting the other men in the congregation know that he would never allow a woman to tell him how to play the tuba.

As the months and years wore on, I focused on simply enabling the teens and adults in our ministry to use their talents to greater effectiveness — putting together new ensembles, coaching soloists, and training the orchestra to accompany the choir for exciting special numbers. Men and women who hadn't played their instruments in decades were dusting them off and seeing God use them to encourage our congregation and our community. We all were blessed by the opportunity to serve God together each week and to watch Him use our efforts as we practiced and rehearsed faithfully.

But that didn't stop the criticism. After only a few years, I decided to turn off my home telephone ringer on Mondays and Thursdays, because after every service someone had to call, "Just to let you know . . ." of some criticism or another. I didn't choose the right hymn (they are always too fast or too slow). I let someone sing that had sinned (because church musicians never should). My clothes were inappropriate (women should always wear a blazer . . . or never should. I couldn't get that right).

Criticism

When the criticism fell on my deaf ears — and my husband was even less receptive — the critics turned to the senior pastor. Nearly every week, a Sunday school teacher or usher or deacon marched into his office to offer helpful suggestions for the orchestra director. He responded by asking me to lead the choir. Now my skirts were too long, then my skirts were too short. The choir numbers were too boring; the music was too peppy. It was enough to make any musician throw in the baton.

It's a sad fact that many men do have a problem with women's roles in the church. It's sad, because the issue really isn't that complicated. We all are commanded to serve the Lord with our talents. We all are commanded to spread the gospel. We all are commanded to love one another. We all are commanded to submit to one another.

It's that word *submission* that so many men and women choke on. One deacon cornered my husband in the back of the auditorium and demanded, "How can *you* allow your wife to lead the choir? I guess we know who wears the pants in your family!"

I wish I had been at his side to see my big, strong Peruvian husband puff out his chest as he gave his firm reply, "You don't think that admitting that she knows more about music than I do means I can't lead in my own home, do you? Well? Do you?" And he chuckled all the way back to the parsonage to tell me how red-faced the man was as he stammered away.

How grieved must God be to see His children still quarreling over who can be the greatest in the church? How sorely must the work of Christ be hindered when we hobble one another with criticism and scorn when we should be lifting one another up? When will we learn to love one another more than the chair we sit in or the stand we perform behind?

It does hurt the congregation when men misappropriate God's role for husband and wife to mean that all women submit to all men. It's unbiblical, it's divisive, and it's contrary to the work of the Spirit. Instead, it's time we all learn Ephesians 5 submission to one another and start serving each other regardless of gender or age or status. It's wrong for the men in the church to prohibit a woman to serve the Lord, and it's just as wrong for a woman to neglect her spiritual gifts because God made her a beautiful lady. God calls us to stop dictating and to start serving.

And that is why women must stop frustrating their own sisters in Christ who are ministering. We cannot tolerate gossip, criticism, and meddling in our congregations. Instead, we need to support one another in word and deed, in prayer and in practice. Since we know firsthand the pressures we all are under, it's easy for us to see the speck in our sister's eye makeup (even if there is a large protruding plank across our own face). Maybe you've experienced some of these less-than-helpful responses from women in the ministry:

- Criticizing your appearance to your face ("I'm sure you would want to know how you look.") or to a friend
- Pointing out the mistakes of your children ("Did you see the spaghetti sauce all over his shirt?")
- Speculating on a friend's marriage ("I can't imagine they are happy at home.")
- Unfaithfulness and unavailability ("That's fine for you to do it because you like it, but I'll just come when I can.")
- Ingratitude ("I'm sure you put a lot of effort into that ministry, but do you really think it made any difference?")

"Do you really think it made any difference?" My friend Carol's words echoed over and over in my head, causing my eyes to burn hot with tears and my chest to tighten with anxiety. Thanking her for the ride home, I excused myself from her van as quickly as politely possible and rushed into the parsonage, locking the door and drawing the shades against the prying eyes and gossiping tongues that seemed ever present.

As I sank to the dingy linoleum, the question reverberated in the small house, mocking the countless hours I had spent on the recent church program. Suddenly, the two repeat performances to a packed auditorium, the hundreds of visitors from the community, the clear presentation of the gospel to souls who needed God's love seemed so trite. In an instant, I forgot the children who had learned to sing Christmas praises to the best of their young, eager abilities, the choir and orchestra members who had faithfully practiced in private and public so they could perform from memory, looking full-faced into the crowd to declare salvation's song. The late nights building sets, the long drama rehearsals repeating the message with increased intensity, the generous donations of costumes, lumber, and cast gifts from church and community members. . . . *Do you really think it makes any difference?*

With a start, as though slapped across the face, I saw the truth. The difference wasn't applause or numbers or achievements or fame. If it were, then obviously the answer was *no. The difference was the work of God.* God's working in the hearts of tired parents who faithfully brought their children to practice, God's working in the hands of business owners and community members who donated to a cause they couldn't understand, God's working in the efforts of simple laymen and women who gave their meager abilities, trusting He would give the increase.

You see, we don't always understand the value of God's work — but God always does. In that one stressed, judgmental congregation, Satan was ripping apart families and friends in their second church split in five years. When, in faith, individuals put aside their personal differences and committed, for just one holiday season, to presenting God's greatest gift to the community, something truly miraculous did happen. The work of God began in our own hearts.

My friend, I don't know what your mantle of ministry looks like today. It may be flashy, or it may appear mundane. It may be brand new with the tags still on it, or it may be worn from much use. And maybe today it feels very heavy, irritating, and hot.

Keep it on.

Put on your coat, walk out the door, and serve. You won't know what the difference is, and your friends may question it to your face. But that doesn't matter. God gave you this ministry, and you will fulfill it beautifully.

What does the Bible say?

Read Ephesians 5 and 6.

What does it mean to you?

Journal your answers and discuss with a friend or your spouse.

1. What does the Bible teach about a woman's ministry within the church? How do you explain that to your daughter? To your friends? To your husband?
2. What is your local church's position on how women serve in the congregation? How does this help or hinder the work in your local community?
3. What ways can you enhance your husband's ministry and enable him to serve more effectively?
4. How are you teaching your children and teens to worship and serve God? How can you better prepare them for services?
5. How does your mantle of ministry feel to you right now? Why?
6. Compare your ministry coat with the armor God gives you in Ephesians 6. What alterations to your ministry coat is the Holy Spirit trying to make?
7. How can you meekly deflect public and private criticism to better focus on the work God has for you to do?
8. Do you save up encouraging notes, thank-you cards, and messages of appreciation from those you serve? How do you practice focusing on the positive results of God's work through you?
9. What ministry (large or small) is God calling you to reach out in faith to serve?

When we show God's
love to others, we
find it for ourselves.

11

Community Influence

I was born in small town Indiana. My parents moved the family when I was seven, so I grew up in the suburbs of Detroit. As an adult, I've lived in an apartment in South Florida, a parsonage on the East Coast, and a two-story brick house here in the Lone Star State. Do you know what all those neighborhoods across the country have in common? Fences.

Robert Frost claims that "good fences make good neighbors," but I've never found that to be the case. Good fences make invisible neighbors. Privacy fences are such a way of life in the Dallas suburbs, you could go your entire life and never see your neighbor's backyard. Without trying, we could pass months without even speaking to the lady next door. These tall wooden fences, leaning with the shifting clay, have become such a part of the landscape that no one gives them a thought. Until one night when they suddenly fall down.

Shortly after dinnertime, when we along with thousands of other families washed up the skillets and stacked the plates into the cabinets, a tornado roared into my town. The emergency sirens blared long and hard, rushing my children to crowd inside the only interior safe room in the house, our tiny half-bathroom (just picture a panicking teen girl, her panting retriever, a swaggering preteen boy, and a crying eight-year-old all huddling around a toilet yelling STOP CRYING at each other). My husband and I, never imagining we could be in any real danger (tornados are the emergencies of *other places,* right?), watched the skies out the front windows as thick clouds covered the normally clear Texas sky and tumultuous winds rattled the windows. Suddenly, we both saw behind the house across the street the horrifying sight of the funnel cloud nearly one mile wide. "Um, David!" I called out, unwilling to further alarm our boisterous children behind me.

"I see it, I'm coming," he answered and rushed to my side. As we squeezed into the closet-sized bathroom with the three children and a dog, the air around us became instantly, terrifyingly quiet. The only sound was the pounding of our hearts as my husband and I stared wordlessly into each other's eyes, each of us remembering the horrific destruction we had witnessed while volunteering for cleanup after a tornado disaster in Oklahoma the year before. How do people walk away unhurt from their home being blown apart? Was I about to find out? The electricity flickered off, then our mobile phones went silent. There was nothing to do but wait with our arms around each other.

"I have to use the bathroom." Everyone groaned, and then piled out of the bathroom to grant my son privacy.

We debated how much longer we should wait to check what was happening outside, but curiosity got the best of us. Cautiously, we opened the front door and stepped outside. Up and down our street, our neighbors were doing the same. Dazed and incredulous, we tested our arms and legs, counted family members and neighbors, then took stock of our homes. The street was littered with trash, branches, and roofing shingles, but miraculously, no one suffered more than minor damage to their homes.

Only a few blocks away, the view was much different. A path of destruction half a mile wide ran for over three miles across town. Over 1,100 homes were damaged or destroyed that night.[1] And on countless streets, fences were blown down and torn apart.

1. Ray Leszcynski, " 'He's Always There': Rowlett Mayor Todd Gottel Hailed for Tornado Response," *The Dallas Morning News,* January 26, 2016, http://www.dallasnews.com/news/community-news/rockwall-rowlett/headlines/20160126-hes-always-there-rowlett-mayor-hailed-for-storm-response.ece.

That night, thousands of residents looked across their demolished fences and began truly getting to know each other. Before the sirens had quieted, neighbors and emergency workers rushed house to house, rescuing families and pets trapped in rubble. People who lived on the opposite side of town posted on the city's Facebook group their addresses with invitations to spend the night in their spare rooms. For weeks afterward, donations poured into churches and civic buildings until the town was so overwhelmed with clothes and toiletries they had to turn items away. Churches housed displaced families and organized volunteer crews. Neighbors came together to help clear paths, sort rubble, and protect belongings. The town social media, often a platform for grumbling or gossiping, became a bulletin board for recovery information, fundraising, pet locating, and sharing prayer requests and praises.

Because when the fences came down, men and women reached out to make a difference.

But now that recovery and rebuilding is underway, one question nags the back of our mind and challenges our return to the status quo: *can we still be good neighbors with good fences?*

When times are good, we easily minimize the importance of community involvement. We are ferociously busy women, charging from management to ministry, homeschool to housework, extracurricular to enrichment activity. We simply don't have time to sit on the front porch and chew the fat. What fat? We run ourselves ragged from sunrise to sunset with not ten minutes to stop and say hello.

So it comes as a shock when we read the story of the good Samaritan in church Sunday morning and begin to identify with the Pharisee and Levite who passed right on by the wounded traveler. They were no doubt running late to Bible study or car pool (donkey pool? Was that a thing?). We don't have time to waste with strangers, do we? Not when we have such important work to do.

And there's the problem. When I allow my schedule to be so full I can't stop to help or say hello to my neighbor, I have declared my to-do list more important than the Great Commission. When I've become so full of ministry programs I can't give of myself to those living around me, I have made my *activities* an idol replacing the One who commanded me to love others.

That's so hard for me to remember. While I do live on a friendly street in a safe neighborhood in the greatest suburb of the best state in the Union, I don't nurture those around me like I should. I'm ashamed to say that there are still some on my street that I wave to as I drive by, wondering what their names are. Wait, is she new here? Or does she live behind me?

To tell you the truth, I thought in all sincerity that I was a very good neighbor. I brought baked goods across the street at Christmas (that one year I baked) and gave rides to the neighbor kids to soccer practice and even opened my home for the preteen boys to have video game tournaments. I organized a block party one weekend last summer, excited to meet a few of the newer neighbors from down the street. Then they introduced themselves, saying they'd lived there over a decade.

Where have I been? Oh, that's right. Inside with the blinds closed, enjoying my own backyard behind the fence.

It is easier than ever to stay behind my fence, too. I have friends at church, my homeschool students have plenty of socialization activities (stop laughing), and I'm more than occupied with my own projects at home. What's more, social media makes it easy to stay in touch with my dear friends across the country and around the world — people who are remarkably like me and who . . . *like me.*

In comparison to that, it can seem very scary to open my own front door, walk across the yard, and knock on my neighbor's door. What will she think? Will she even open the door? What if she mentions the weeds in the yard or my loud children or that leaning fence? On second thought, I'll shut the door and go back to Facebook.

I'm glad my own neighbors didn't feel the same way. Instead, they modeled for me and for my children *what it means to be a good neighbor,* and by hesitantly following their example, we gained rich relationships that changed us more than them.

They Came Outside

The quiet Mexican lady across the street did something every day for a couple years that I thought was so odd. Every afternoon, she stood at the bottom of her driveway, just watching her children riding their bikes and kicking the soccer ball around. She remained there for a couple of hours, sometimes bringing a chair and sitting. She was just there. It was so weird. I watched her from behind the curtain, then told my husband about this odd behavior. He then said something that blew my mind. "You should go out sometime and talk to her."

Hesitantly, I stepped out one afternoon with my baby on my hip and lamely tried to start a conversation. "Our children are about the same age," I stammered. She smiled and started pointing and naming and giving ages, and I did the same. She asked a question, I answered and asked her a question, and lo and behold, we struck up a conversation!

Pretty soon, I was watching out the window for her to come out so I could go say hi again. "Hello, Neighbor!" she called enthusiastically. "I can't remember names, so I just call you Neighbor!" With relief, I knew she would be my friend forever; I can't remember my own children's names.

Our boys became best friends. I bring her sons to soccer practice sometimes, and she brings me homemade tamales. After a few years, we actually learned each other's names, husband's names, routines, and favorite drinks. All because she was standing outside.

They Checked on Us

Soon after we moved in, we had some seriously disgusting plumbing issues that I promise I'll never tell you about and for that you will remain grateful. So there were plumbers' vans in front of the house several times. And some anxious digging around the front yard. And some ominous machine rentals from Home Depot®. And some odor. At each sign of trouble, the doorbell rang. And there was the neighbor, asking if we were ok and if we needed anything and if we would like a phone or a recommendation or a bathroom or a glass of water or a wet vac. We learned early and often since we moved here that *neighbors care*. They watch out and they reach out before they are asked.

My children learned that quickly from the men and women around them on the street. They appreciate so much knowing that there are so many who care about them, people whose doors they can literally knock on and get help anytime. That's why my son is the first to know about late-night ambulance visits, following up to see if anyone needs support or someone to walk the dog or just to hold a hand and pray.

One afternoon, that son came running to me with his eyes wide with fear. "I hear Mrs. B screaming outside! Something's wrong!" I followed him to the front door in disbelief, but the sound outside filled me with terror. Blood-curdling shrieks came from within the house next door, and my first thought was that someone must be inside attacking her.

So I ran, barefoot and empty-handed, right inside her house. "Where are you? What happened?" I yelled, then wondered how I would fight off a criminal with no weapon of my own. Maybe my panicky, high-pitched voice would intimidate the attacker? I felt really, really silly. Then I saw her.

"Help me! Oh, please help me!" she sobbed from the edge of her bed. As I crossed the bedroom, I shuddered involuntarily. My normally beautiful neighbor was contorted in pain, clutching her arm and screaming. Through her bare shoulder I could clearly see her upper arm bone was out of position, protruding through her chest. My stomach lurched, but I willed myself to remain calm and not freak out by repeating over and over in my mind that at least it wasn't, as I first imagined, blood and guts.

With a deep breath, I found my Mommy voice and calmly took control of the situation. Don't look at the arm. Put shoes on her. Move the van to her driveway. Tell the teen to watch the younger children. Drive her to the hospital down the street. Don't look at the arm. Carry her purse. Distract her with small talk. Pray aloud. Don't look at the arm.

In a few minutes, she was in a private ER room, getting shots to ease the pain and an X-ray to survey the damage. Every time someone touched her arm or asked about the injury, she was overcome with the pain and horror, so I endeavored to keep her mind on other things. I asked about her childhood. She told me how she met her husband. She recalled funny stories from her career in the makeup industry. And with each recurring wave of pain, she would look up and pray aloud to Jesus, begging Him to help her endure. We talked for hours until her husband arrived. By then, she was in a sling, well-dosed-up on pain killers, and quite calm.

That incident drew us together. Her bravery and faith in the midst of such a tortuous injury inspired me to look beyond my petty annoyances. I insisted on taking her to her follow-up appointments with the surgeon just to glean more from her testimony, gaining makeup advice, product samples, and a renewed vision for passionate prayer.

A year or so later when my heart heaved in pain from a bullying friend, the stories my neighbor had told me right there in the ER came back to mind. I knew my neighbor understood, had overcome, and had seen God work through similar circumstances. So again, I ran across the grass and bolted through her front door, but this time I was the one screaming in pain. And she was there, patting a space for me on the bed beside her to rest while she calmly reminded me of God's grace. She distracted me from the present pain to look up again, and to look forward to the healing Jesus was working in my life. Don't look at the pain; look at Jesus.

I wonder if that's really God's plan for loving our neighbors. Sure, we have safer streets and greener plants when we are looking in on each other. It's nice to have someone to walk the dog when we're out of town or to let us know about break-ins in the area. But that's not the real reason we reach out to our neighbors. We reach across the fence and across the street because when we show God's love to others, we find it for ourselves.

We find God's love over baked beans at the block party, while learning guitar chords in the garage, from helping the shut-ins with the yard work. We catch it while buying the children's fundraising candies and asking about the new job. We witness it while we watch the neighborhood children come together to clear brush in front of the abandoned house. We feel it up close at the neighbor child's concert or sporting event. We touch it sitting by the hospital bed and attending the funeral.

Christ wanted the Pharisees and Levites and religious people and me to know that being a good neighbor is so much more than cutting the lawn and running the charity and obeying the law. It's even harder than fixing the destroyed fence. Being a good neighbor is actually touching one another, really looking at each other, and truly crying with one another.

A good neighbor is love.

What does the Bible say?

Read Luke 10 and Ephesians 4.

What does it mean to you?

Journal your answers and discuss with a friend or your spouse.

1. How many of your neighbors do you know by name? Write them down and pray for them today.
2. Who on your street have you not met? How can you be neighborly this week?
3. What needs are represented on your street, in your neighborhood, in your town? How are you helping to meet those needs?
4. Are you involved yet? Find a project, volunteer organization, or charity in your town to volunteer with for a short time. See what a difference it makes in your perspective.
5. Are your children involved in the lives of others? Help them reach out by making crafts, doing yard work, and visiting shut-ins on a regular basis.

Shining forth God's glory, displaying His image, and demonstrating His love and compassion may be just the purpose He has for me right now.

12

True Compassion

Nothing compares to the exhilaration of childbirth, when the pain and purgatory of pregnancy gives way to the blessed reality of a warm, wailing body released from the womb to snuggle close to the heart. We dream of this moment as little girls, we pray for it as young wives, then we eagerly anticipate it as expectant mothers. So many prayers, so much planning and researching and purchasing go into that one moment, the culmination of a young family's hopes and dreams for the future.

But no one prepares us for what comes next. After nine months of pregnancy and a hard day and night of labor, the cruel irony of the Curse leaves the triumphant new mother bruised and battered, ill-prepared to return to her own responsibilities, let alone to take on the care and feeding of a helpless newborn.

My first pregnancy was longer and harder than I could have imagined, compounded with a rare and undiagnosed complication that would render me bedridden for each of my following three pregnancies. In eager anticipation for childbirth, my pelvic bones excitedly false-start months too soon, pulling out of joint against my will and the advice of my physicians. The only cure is childbirth, but, alas, babies appreciate remaining within the womb until fully baked and the red button pops out indicating they are done. So pregnant me has nothing to do but attempt to distract myself from the sword-like pain shooting between my legs by counting down the days and hours until my obstetrician gives the green light for relief.

There is no mother anywhere on the earth who looks forward to giving birth as much as I do. Labor is a walk in the park after staggering the halls and leaning over a walker in excruciating pain for months on end. Like a POW dreaming of release, I only imagine beautiful, pain-free days and long, sleep-full nights.

And that is exactly *not* what comes after giving birth, is it? My first baby didn't sleep more than an hour at a time the first two days. Eighteen hours of hard labor had left me weak and surprisingly hormonal (why didn't anyone tell me I would feel like a monster?). I couldn't stand up straight since my bones had not yet returned to their fore-ordained positions. And my long labor had left my face so hideously bruised and swollen, the nurses kept the mirrors covered for two days so I wouldn't see myself and freak out.

My poor, young husband dragged me home to our second-floor apartment (how did he get me and the baby upstairs?), and found himself ill-equipped to juggle my mood swings and our oversized newborn's voracious appetite all at once. Fortunately for him, we were too poor for paternity leave; he ran out the door the next day with a kiss and a sigh of relief. Weakly, I pulled the baby into bed with me and took turns nursing him and crying. This was no way to begin Happily Ever After.

To add insult to injury, the next day I had to take our heir-apparent to the pediatrician for a weigh-in and jaundice check. Since my husband drove our only car to work, he asked his mother to come check on me and take me to the appointment. I was mortified; the last thing I wanted at that moment was to allow my mother-in-law to see me in such a fragile physical and emotional state. My temper was worn thin, I had no hope of ever using the restroom again, and my chest had swollen to several times its natural size. There was not a system in my body that was working for my beautification at that moment, and I could not even imagine ever feeling happy or comfortable again. But with no wheels of my own and little ability to stagger across the room holding onto the wall, I had no other alternatives. I was completely at the mercy of the mother-in-law.

Mid-morning, the front door of my apartment opened. "Lea AAAAAnn! Good Moooorning!" Raquel sang through my open bedroom door. "I will take you to your doctor now. Let me help you!" Her Spanish accent rolled thick with eager cheerfulness.

I sighed with heavy resignation. If my husband and I display opposite personalities in every way, my mother-in-law and I are different species altogether. Every introverted, introspective, reflective instinct within me is countered with her outgoing, demonstrative, optimistic personality. We rarely ever have the same opinion on any subject. So while every cell within me screamed to crawl into a hole and pull the hole in after me, she marched through my bedroom and physically yet happily propelled me outside into the South Florida sunshine.

Fortunately for both of us, she is a strong woman. With one hand, she carried the baby in his car seat carrier, while with the other she half-pulled and half-dragged me and my oversized diaper bag down the stairs and into the car. Between my pessimistic mechanical observations and her dogged enthusiasm, we managed to get the baby seat strapped into the back of her Toyota. But then came me. My difficult pregnancy and a hard labor had left me far less than limber; I could not yet sit at a 90-degree angle. It took the two of us to wedge me half standing and half sitting sideways into the front passenger seat of the compact sedan and weave the seat belt around my frame. Getting the baby and me into the car had taken us nearly a half an hour.

Running around the car to the driver's side, Raquel hopped in and switched on the motor. "We'll be a little late, but we'll make it!" She turned to me with a wide smile, then furrowed her brow in concern. "Um, Lea Ann, dear, have you fed the baby lately?"

"I had just finished nursing him when you came. Why?"

"Well, honey, and I say this with all my love, you look like you need to nurse him again. Are you hurting?"

I looked down to see the front of my shirt bulging before me like Dolly Parton's blouse — if Dolly Parton had taken part in a wet T-shirt competition. After spraying herself with sour dairy products. "I've changed my shirt three times this morning!" I wailed. "And I am *always* hurting!" I started to cry, wondering if my tears could wash away the stinky milk stains down my front.

"Of course you do. This is so hard right now, and I don't know why Americans make young mothers go out of the house when you just gave birth. At least in Peru, my doctor had the sense to come to me." She deftly turned onto the highway. "But, never mind. The pediatrician will completely understand, so don't be embarrassed. And when we come home, I'll help you feel better. Have you heard of using cabbage? No? I know you don't believe me, but cabbage will make it all feel better. You'll see. Just put your head back and try to rest and everything will be better soon."

As I feared, we were very late to the appointment. And my shirt reeked. And the baby soiled the examining table. And the infant scale verified that my bulging chest had been doing a good job so far. Raquel was right; the nursing staff and doctors were all kind and congratulatory while all I could think about was getting back to the apartment and ripping my fast-tightening shirt off of myself and crawling back into bed. She was more than happy to show off the baby to all the nurses first, however, bragging about the delivery and vital signs while I leaned weakly against the wall and tried not to think about my painful upper-body swelling.

At last, Raquel triumphantly wedged the baby seat and my swollen, weakening mass back into her Toyota to transport us back to the apartment. Thoughtfully, she deposited me in my bed, changed the baby again, and handed him to me before leaving for the grocery store. I painfully nursed on my side, praying blessings on the maternity nurse who had taught me how to feed the baby lying down, and wondered if I would ever become immune to the sickening smell of rotten milk that had become my new signature scent.

When I opened my eyes a few hours later, the apartment glowed in the magically golden late-afternoon tropical sun. The baby wasn't beside me, but when I raised my head, I caught a glimpse of him softly snoring in his Pack 'n Play® to my left. Through my open bedroom door, I could see the apartment clutter had been cleared away, though a few sacks of groceries remained on the pass-through counter. "Did I wake you?" Raquel's slight form bounced into the doorway. "I think the cabbage is ready. Let me show you what to do with it."

I shuddered. *Cabbage? Why must I be tortured with bitter vegetables at a time like this? Have I not been through enough?*

Raquel softly padded into the room carrying a steaming platter of bright green leaves. "They didn't have the red ones, but these should work just as well." For the sake of familial harmony and in the spirit of gratitude for her help that morning, it had to be done. I leaned my head back onto my pillow and closed my eyes in resignation. If eating bitter herbs was what it took, I would just get it over with as quickly as possible. Maybe the fiber would help my postpartum bathroom problems, after all. My husband was definitely going to hear about this when he returned home.

"Lift your shirt." I stared blankly at my mother-in-law, unsure if our language barrier was rising again. Seeing my hesitation, she stepped forward. "Your arms must be sore from the swelling. Just lay back, and I'll do it."

Frozen to the bed in shock, I watched my petite Hispanic mother-in-law lift my shirt and place steaming hot cabbage leaves over my swollen breasts as a warm poultice. In one deep breath, I inwardly laughed at my own foolishness and relaxed in comfort. The relief was nearly instantaneous. In a half an hour, my bedsheets were a mess of water and milk, but my torso was closer to normal size and I had regained the use of my upper arms. It was a Peruvian miracle.

But just as suddenly as she had appeared, Raquel was gone, leaving me to catch up on my rest until David returned. When he did, he was surprised to find not only his wife lying in bed lucid and pleasant, but his refrigerator full and his supper warm on the stove.

Over the next year, the swift and meaningful Peruvian miracle would occur at just the right time: a sack of groceries, a dinner invitation, a spare twenty dollars, an evening of babysitting. I was often amazed at her uncanny ability to sense what I needed before I even knew it. For a woman so different from me, she sure knew me. Whenever I needed a mother the most, she did what she could to comfort, protect, and provide for me until I was strong enough to mother myself.

It was years before I understood the secret to the Peruvian miracle. My mother-in-law knew what I was going through because her early years as a young mother were shockingly similar to mine.

On the other side of the equator a generation earlier, Raquel struggled daily with her own relationship with her mother. Things came to a head when she ran away to marry, but she soon found herself juggling multiple babies in poverty with little family support.

So when I had my first baby (her seventh or eighth grandchild), she remembered what it was like to be lonely, scared, and stressed. She recalled how difficult it was to learn how to parent when she still needed a mother, herself. She had felt the fear of the unknown when she blazed her own trail, becoming the mother she had never experienced. She knew how to demonstrate compassion, because she had borne the pain. She remembered what it felt like to cry through her own painfully spilled milk.

Passing on the Compassion

My mother-in-law knew that the pain we experience in life should fuel our compassion. God comforts us in our painful trials so that we can pass the same hope on to others (2 Corinthians 1:4). Indeed, compassion for those around us demonstrates our Christ-like love and obedience to God's commands (Galatians 6:2; 1 Peter 3:18). We know God expects us to reach out in compassion, and we desperately need others to reach out to *us* when we are needy.

We know this, but living it out every day is surprisingly difficult. Why is it so hard to demonstrate compassion? Why is love rarely my default reaction to someone unlike me, someone needy or struggling, someone difficult to relate to or understand?

When it comes down to it, my default reaction is much more fleshly. I can be judgmental (Why can't she get her act together?) or petty (Is she really allowing her child to wear that to church?). I easily take offense (Oh, no, she did *not* just say that to me!) and can be downright harsh (Hmph. You know what she *really* meant by that?!).

I'm so dependent upon compassion that I greedily hoard it for myself. I treasure within my memory and deep recesses of my heart every mention of God's love and forgiveness and care, certain each verse was written just to me.

Only me.

But the woman across the aisle at church, across the street from my house, down the bench from me at the soccer game *is just as loved by God*, just as needy and vulnerable and reliant on His mercy. While I'm selfishly demanding others cut me some slack, I'm not as generous handing out the mercy to others.

That's why keeping the two Greatest Commandments is so desperately impossible. I cannot dethrone myself completely from my own life, for this wretched, cursed self is ever-present until Jesus comes. This warfare waging daily in my heart drives me, like the apostle Paul, to hurl myself at the foot of the Cross and plead for deliverance (Romans 7:24). Deliver me from idolatry, Lord! Deliver me from sin and selfishness and small-mindedness! Renew within me a love for Yourself and compassion for Your children!

That renewal Paul outlines in Romans 8 is the key to my relationship not only with God, but also with my fellow man. To replace my own natural instincts of judgment and pride and selfishness with love, compassion, and giving requires a complete mind and heart transplant. And that's what Paul describes. My own sinful, cursed state shrivels up my soul, disfiguring the image of God within me. God's work of sanctification changes my depraved will and my flesh-driven inner man from this sinful, cursed state that I am in. I'm God's fixer-upper, transforming into the image of Christ, back to what I was always intended to be.

As I allow the Holy Spirit to control and renew my mind, will, and emotions, the glory of God shines forth. This glorious beauty shines with an active radiance, God's own self *verbing* through me: loving, forgiving, serving, sacrificing, reaching, touching, healing. I desperately need this newness, a return to Eden's plan and purpose for imaging the Godhead here on earth.

To reach out and serve in meaningful compassion toward those around me who desperately need God's love, I desperately need God's renewing Spirit to reign in my heart. I need Christ before I can give Christ.

I need God to change me, then I need God to open my eyes to those around me in need of His love. My life, my schedule, my to-do list, my fatigue, and my busyness cloud my vision constantly. I need to open my eyes to God's golden sunlight falling on those around me who need His healing.

Am I too busy to help? Do I prioritize serving others like I do keeping my appointments or finishing my to-do list or documenting my children's homeschooling? I don't — not often enough. My responsibilities are, after all, quite important. I simply must keep the children fed and the house (relatively) clean and the homeschooling "on track" (whatever that means) and the errands run. But what about the rest of God's will for my life? Could not shining forth His glory, displaying His image, and demonstrating His love and compassion be just the purpose He has for me right now?

I know that one hot, sunny September day my mother-in-law was right where God placed her — at my side even when I didn't know I wanted her there. She had other things to do, a job and obligations and friends and family members who depended on her. But that day, she did God's work in our apartment.

It must not have been easy for her to slip into a role no one served for her. While she lugged my baggage and heavy body around the parking lot and through the medical office, she must have remembered that no one had carried her through post-partum care. When she ran my errands and cooked my dinner and poulticed my chest, she may have recalled struggling through those tasks on her own. Surely the event conjured up those feelings of loneliness, abandonment, and loss. She chose to overcome bitterness with service.

Showing compassion brings us face to face with our own pain. To truly love someone in their trial, we must put ourselves in their shoes. If we have actually worn those shoes before in real life, that is a harsh experience. How much easier to simply turn away, to ignore the situation and the painful memories it brings back. We don't want to pick at our wound, to poke at the barely healed scar.

But that self-centered reaction to pain denies the glorious deliverance. The fact that we have any measure of healing reveals the work of grace within our hearts. All of creation is groaning together, desperately needing this miraculous healing (Romans 8:22), yet we all have the same *hope.* The hope that shines forth in each of us grants healing from our painful pasts, and that hope is what we can share with others — the chicken soup of hope in God's deliverance from pain, the cabbage of God's healing placed over the heart.

Meaningful, healing, restorative compassion hurts not only because of our own limitations and our own pain. Compassion costs us; it is a sacrifice. God's compassion on our sin caused Him to sacrifice His own life for the opportunity to "freely give us all things" (Romans 8:31). Giving all the things is expensive. It requires a generous, hilarious love that is so radical, so counter-cultural that we must fight hard for it. And the battleground remains within our hearts.

We fight within our hearts for compassion because, again, our natural inclination is to hoard the good things: the good things of love, of worth, of meaning, of compassion. We desperately need these, urgently seek them every day, and store them up for ourselves. Intentionally living and breathing God's image, however, demands sacrificial love for those around us, those hurting people we brush past and scurry around every day. Romans 8 compassion is spiritually minded life-giving, confident inheritance-claiming, "God is for us" compassion. It is turning aside from condemnation and grasping new life for ourselves and for others. It is facing our own failures with humility when we find the downtrodden Samaritan, rather than hurrying away in self-righteous pride and judgment.

If that sounds a lot like forgiveness, that's because it is. We own a new life, new meaning, new hope because God forgave us and declared boldly that He is for us. We give new life, new meaning, and new hope to those around us when we display His forgiveness and His power toward them.

To minister compassionately, we first must avail ourselves of God's forgiveness on our behalf. There is no condemnation now — our sins, our mistakes, our failings, our inadequacies are all covered at the Cross. When God looks at us, He doesn't see the teen pregnancies and the failed marriages, the dropped schooling and the job losses, the past addictions and crimes. He doesn't hold the hurtful words, broken relationships, and missed opportunities over our head. He forgives us, He gives us life, and He renews our spirit every day because *God is for us* (Romans 8:31).

Serving with compassion means forgiving myself as God forgave me, and it also means extending that forgiveness to those who wronged me. We cannot hold out our hands in hope if our arms remain full of the burdens of bitterness. And this is hard. Some burdens we must lay down at the Cross daily, over and over begging God to take care of the abusers and the bullies who painfully stomp over God's image on our lives. Instead, we beg the Christ within us to provide new life, new vision, and new hope for their reconciliation (Romans 8:11–13).

Finally, compassionate love forgives the ones we serve. I am humbled to recall Raquel's care for me while I was petty and pouting. I didn't want her around that day, and I did not radiate thankfulness and love toward her by any means. But she loved me anyway, forgiving my cranky attitude and sour disposition (and even the smell). Like the Holy Spirit in Romans 8:26, she knew what I really needed before I could even ask for help. She demonstrated Christ-like compassion, exemplifying love toward me when I didn't even want it.

True compassion demands more than monetary donations and food pantries. Compassion costs more than just a few volunteer hours or a hot meal. Biblical, lasting, life-giving compassion requires giving ourselves, sacrificing the God image within us for the love and hope for someone else. God is for us, and we must be for our neighbor, too.

What does the Bible say?

Read Romans 7:7–8:39 and Galatians 6.

What does it mean to you?

Journal your answers and discuss with a friend.

1. When has someone's compassion for you changed your day?
2. How often do you recognize the needs around you? What brings them to your attention?

3. Who came to your mind while you were reading this chapter? Why?
4. Is there a past pain that hinders your love for someone? Who do you need to forgive?
5. What should compassion cost you? How are you preparing to pay that price?
6. What acts of compassion will you fulfill this week?

To live within my
means, I must remain
plugged into the
power of the
Holy Spirit.

13

The Time Budget

I can't coupon. I play the violin, teach algebra, and speak Starbucks® fluently, but I cannot for the life of me coupon. I'm a soccer mom, a homeschool mom, a music mom, and a blogging mom, but I'll never be a money-saving mom. It's not gonna happen.

My friend across town is a coupon queen. She collects thick binders full of coupons, she sends envelopes of refund forms regularly, she shops several different stores each week for the very best deals, and she saves tens of thousands of dollars on groceries and household items every year. I don't understand her at all.

I get confused as soon as I enter a grocery store, emerging an hour later with half the items on my list, a headache, and the distinct impression I have been taken advantage of. I'm convinced there is a trick with the lighting and air ventilation systems inside these buildings that renders normally logical, clear-headed people insane when they enter those automatic sliding doors. If I go to the grocery store unattended, I'm sure to get lost within the first couple of hours and require assistance finding my way out. Two years ago, my favorite grocery store rearranged the shelves "to serve you better." I cried. I haven't found the ketchup since.

To serve us better, my husband does the grocery shopping for our family. We need food, we need to have some money left over after buying the food, and we need me to retain my mental faculties.

So he's the food procurer, and I'm the food cooker and eater. The system works really well for us.

My husband is not an extreme couponer, but he has a good head for the grocery game. He remembers the prices for most items in our three main grocery stores in town, and he has a system for buying what we need at the least cost. Armed with my list of ingredients for the coming week, he can blow into first one store and then another, grabbing only what is the best deal from that grocery before dropping the bags off at home and dashing to the next store. He will complete two or three different stops in less than two hours, and even pick up surprises I didn't ask for like a bouquet of flowers or pound of sliced goat cheese or bacon. He's so hot.

If we want to eat well and still pay the mortgage, we have to learn to *budget our grocery spending.* We need to buy all the things like chicken legs and almond milk and apples and toilet paper and lipstick and still have money left for graphic T-shirts and books. That's called *adulting* our money. And one way or another, through a lot of trial and error, we figure it out over time and come up with a system that works for us, whether it is coupon binders or cost comparison booklets or sending our own hot Latino to navigate the sales. We learn how to budget our money for our survival and enjoyment, and we figure out how to make what is most important fit onto our debit card, and we finally know instinctively that some things are only for rare occasions, like that huge one-pound brie and flank steak. I don't mourn flank steak anymore, because I've learned it isn't worth it to spend half my budget on one meal, and I can use a different cut that will be plenty tasty and still leave me money for Tuesday's tacos.

I cannot for the life of me keep a mental tally of what I'm purchasing and a map of the store and a comparison of other retailers all in my brain at the same time. I am not gifted in stretching a dollar. I am, however, increasingly adept at stretching an *hour,* and my special superpower is juggling responsibilities.

Managing Our Time Budget

We moms understand the importance of the grocery budget, but we find it so much harder to manage our *time budget.* We fall into the 12-year-old mentality that resources are limitless and all good opportunities are equally awesome. So at the end of the day, and periodically through the year, we find ourselves blowing our budget on the wrong items, leaving us bankrupt of energy, creativity, joy, and even the will to go on.

In the rush to get it all done, we forget that seemingly obvious truth that *time is finite.* We only have a limited number of hours in a day, days in a year, and years in our lifetime. It's a sobering fact that we drive out of our minds but we can never erase, for God has written down the limit of our time on earth, a boundary we cannot pass beyond (Job 14:5; Psalm 139:16). Our stewardship, our responsibility with this budget of time we have been entrusted, is to spend it wisely (Psalm 90:10–12).

As a child, I became enamored with a quote from Benjamin Franklin: "Dost thou love life? Then do not squander time, for that is the stuff life is made of." There were many things that the young me could not control (how much control does a child have on their own life?), but I could manage my time. If I wanted more time to do what I wanted — reading books on my bed or riding my bike to my friend Sarah's house — then I had to carefully control my time and obligations. I began setting my alarm clock one, then two hours earlier than the rest of my family so I could have a private devotional time, memorize AWANA® verses, read a chapter or two of a novel, shower, dress, eat breakfast, and study for an upcoming test before the day began in earnest. I eagerly sought out spare time to reclaim, reading textbooks in the car during errands and rushing through homework during my sister's music lessons.

When I attended college, I found my time-reclaiming skills put to the test. I had to squeeze my necessary tasks like practicing and homework and laundry around inconvenient class and rehearsal schedules. I started practicing poor budgeting by working through meal times and eating Little Debbie® snacks on my way to rehearsal. I woke early to finish my homework and intentionally slept during easy classes. The more reckless my schedule became, the more dissatisfaction I felt. Subjects I enjoyed and activities that should have energized me instead became a burden; I lost my love for learning, for music, and for my friends.

That same pattern has followed me through life. I remain an expert *schedule packer*; I should create a Pinterest image about how to fit a week's worth of activities into one overnight space. But when I start recklessly throwing obligations and activities willy-nilly into my calendar, my inner self is crushed, wrinkled, and creased from the strain. I become hurried, then stressed, then cranky, then ill, then deeply unhappy. My close friends and family look on with concern, sincerely begging me to lighten my load to regain serenity.

I've come to realize through a couple of decades of trial and error that too many obligations, too much to do, isn't really the problem. The problem is that I'm spending my time budget haphazardly, throwing items into my cart without first considering how I will pay for them. If I'm shopping for activities and interests without first accounting for the necessities, I am overextended by the end of the month and dissatisfied with my standard of living. I'm scheduling above my means.

Living within our means, managing our responsibilities and to-do list and relationships and interests doesn't mean giving up everything. Instead, wise stewardship takes into account what necessities must be spent (self-care, marriage, child rearing, home maintenance, work), what budget we are working with, and how we want to invest our discretionary funds. It's making intentional choices to create a life of meaningful impact.

This is where the false metaphor of *balance* fails us as women. We know that our grocery budget is rarely balanced. Some weeks we spend a lot on cleaning supplies and toilet paper, because it all runs out at the same time. For months on end, baby diapers, formula, and detergent eat up the large chunk of every paycheck. There are weeks we only buy flu medicine, chicken soup, Lysol®, and tissues. It is actually very rare that the conveyor belt in the checkout line is evenly balanced with healthy food, meat, dairy products, and household supplies. But what we do purchase is budgeted, and we expect every week, month, and year to look a little different.

Our time budget, too, should be just as flexible. When we recognize our time not as a pie chart to color into neat tenths of activity, but instead view our days as a budget we spend according to our priorities and needs, we can confidently spend each hour on what matters most. When I understood that, when I viewed my calendar as a stewardship to budget, I immediately experienced *freedom* to manage my budget joyfully.

I'm not going to tell you how to budget your time any more than I'm going to prescribe what you should buy from Target this week, because we are all unique, and we all have different styles and desires and priorities. I can't stand spending money on toilet paper; I just hate using money that I could be investing in coffee on a commodity I will flush. But I have a friend who will only buy really soft TP because she hates anything scratchy touching her person. She saves money by purchasing cheap coffee. I can't bring myself to do that. Neither of us is more spiritual than the other, we just budget for what matters to us. Our time is the same way.

Prioritizing Our Time

Our big investment — the mortgage payment of our time — is for *relationships.* Though each of us have different needs and circumstances, we have learned to live within our housing means, and we need to be as intentional with the most important people in our lives. Just like we pay the mortgage or rent first every month, we need to prioritize our time with family and friends.

I was thinking of that recently when discussing *date night* with some friends. My husband and I place a very, very high priority on date night; we haven't missed a single week since the first year of our marriage. Though now we frequently enjoy dinner and a movie or attend an event downtown, in our early years date night meant pizza out of the box on the floor in front of the TV. Whatever we do, we know that there is set aside a serious block of time once a week where we just talk about what's on our minds, share our fears and anxieties, plan our shared future, and hug and kiss. Date night is a really big deal for us. Reserving that time for our relationship each week is how we demonstrate our ongoing commitment to one another.

Some of my friends have great marriages without a standing date night. They prioritize their time together in different ways — coffee each morning or evening walks or late-night chats on the sofa or reading together. The main thing is to budget the marriage intentionally, and to always pay it first.

As our family has grown, budgeting for each child has become increasingly important. If I don't purposefully seek out time with each one, I can easily find myself treating them as a herd that just needs to be shuffled from place to place. Instead, I want each of my children and teens to know that they are loved for the unique, fascinating person they are individually. That takes an investment of time.

For the last year, I began budgeting my time with friends as a priority, as well. I realize more than ever my need for encouragement, counsel, and prayer from those around me, and I want to have that same uplifting effect on them, too. So I have set aside regular time to meet for dinner or coffee or a walk in the park with several different ladies, and this habit has made a tremendous difference in my perspective.

The single most critical relationship I budget, however, is with God. It pains me that when life becomes hurried and hectic, it's often my morning devotions that are slept through or my evening prayers that are swept aside. That is poor management, like not paying the power bill in the midst of a Texas summer. It makes no sense, but my sin nature is not usually logical. To live within my means, I must remain plugged into the power of the Holy Spirit.

After I carefully budget the most important relationship expenditures, I am ready to move on to the *health care* account. We all carefully plan our health insurance and medical spending account, and we save a little more for those unplanned illnesses, extra tissue boxes, and ER visits. We fund these budgets not only for medical bills, but also for preventive care and unexpected illness, knowing the health and safety of our loved ones is the priority.

Taking Care of Our Own Needs

My own spiritual, emotional, and physical health needs to be that much of a priority to me. I'm no good to anyone if I'm too overwrought, sick, and stressed to care for myself or others. So while emergencies, accidents, and tragedies happen, I want to do all I can to plan ahead to be at my best. That's what wise self-care is all about.

I'm not advocating laziness or self-indulgence, but we must avoid irresponsibility and burnout. Wise stewardship mandates budgeting for our long-term health.

Physical health needs to be a budget item, as much as I don't enjoy it. You won't find anyone who hates exercise, diet, and doctor's appointments as much as I do, but I do try to budget time every day to improve my own health. It's a constant battle that I'm not ready to give up yet.

Keeping my diet healthy, moving my sedentary self off the chair, and sleeping a sound seven or eight hours every night are all *musts* for just maintaining my physical health. They even work wonders for my mental and emotional health. I also cut out on discouraging, tense, or over-stimulating books and movies that drag my spirit down.

Budgeting my self-care also means looking ahead for pitfalls. When I know that certain situations or activities are particularly draining, I schedule time for rest and recuperation. After a major holiday, performance, or project, it is common on our family calendar to have a bold DAY OF REST scheduled, during which no one may commit Mom to anything. Too much excitement and too many people quickly deplete my energy, and I will require extra fresh air, deep sleep, and nutritious meals to recharge. I've learned that budgeting these rests ahead of time actually helps me bounce back faster and saves hard feelings in our home.

Being a wife, a mom, a homeschooler, a ministry leader, and a woman is exhausting, and we need refreshment. Part of my self-care health budget includes special times of relaxation. Once a year, my husband and I try to get away for a weekend to see new sights, reconnect with each other, and just enjoy a change of pace. I also enjoy traveling for brief visits on my own, visiting family members or friends out of state and reconnecting with who I am outside the house. Just a few days away sufficiently resets my spirit so that I'm missing my family and ready to return to the daily grind. For me, getting away from it all is an important budget item. For others, it's a special treat, like filet mignon, reserved for rare occasions. Regardless, the importance of self-care cannot be over-emphasized. Our time budget must include this insurance policy.

After the relationships and self-care are accounted for, we still have multiple responsibility bills to pay. There are some we dread and may try to cancel, but most of them are coming back regularly for the duration. These jobs, ministries, and volunteer projects make up the bulk of our calendar items and to-do lists. We have homeschooling, carpooling, work in the home and out of the home, sports practices, and errands to run. We serve in church nursery, Sunday school class, and potlucks. We head up fundraisers and champion social causes. It all takes time and energy, loading up our cart and quickly depleting our budget.

Just like my grocery confusion leads to throwing things willy-nilly into my cart in an anxious attempt to get out of there, emotions often fuel my time debt. I'm afraid to disappoint, I am driven by guilt, and I don't want to say *no.* So I take on more and more until, once again, I'm overcommitted and scheduled above my means.

Being in debt doesn't do my family any financial favors; we recognize the opportunities and blessings that are missed when we are strapped for cash. Indeed, one of the biggest motivations for Christians to eliminate debt is to *regain the ability to give generously.* And the same holds true for our time budget. When we allow ourselves to overextend the calendar, stuffing more into each day or week than our budget can cover, we eliminate the opportunity to reach out and give of ourselves spontaneously. We may even find ourselves so strapped for resources that we borrow from the energy or health accounts, jeopardizing our most important relationships and our own well-being.

This is why regular accounting is imperative. Extra obligations and expenditures sneak in every week, and many of them remain legitimate investments of our time budget. However, if we don't periodically examine our budget and compare our actual expenditures with the reality of our habits, we could slide into debt unintentionally. I take a personal accounting twice a year — every January 1 and every fall (before the new homeschool year). These are two natural *beginnings* that motivate me to start fresh, to clear out dead weight, and to recommit myself to the work God designed me to complete.

When accounting season comes, I take some time to examine my life in private. I'll spend extra time in prayer and Bible reading, entreating God to lead my decisions and to reveal the changes He desires in me. I then journal about what blessings I am experiencing and what burdens trouble my spirit. I will list the important relationships that God has entrusted me with, as well as the obligations I have taken on. I will assess my own physical, emotional, and spiritual health, listing any issues that are troubling me. Finally, I will dig out my resolutions or goals from the previous accounting to compare what I had *intended* against how I was actually *living* several months later.

I usually find a few things that are better than I thought and some areas that show distinct improvement. But every time I go through this accounting, the Lord reveals *debts* that I had not realized were accruing — obligations I should not have signed up for, projects that were outside my budget, and investments that were neglected.

Since I err on the side of taking too much on, January and August have become great times to *quit things.* That is not easy to do. I think we all want to be dependable; the kind of women people can count on to *get it done*. But in reality, not every one of us can do everything. I need to leave some for you to do, and you leave some things for me to do. That's being the Body of Christ.

In an ideal life, we will never get into time debt because we will say *no* to the unnecessary extras. Saying *no* is very hard to do; this is why we try not to go grocery shopping when we are hungry or when cookies are on sale. Being prepared, satisfied, and confident helps us make wise decisions when we are confronted with tempting opportunities.

This regular accounting every few months builds satisfaction and direction into our time budget. When we know we have budgeted our time and energy for the most important pursuits, the tasks that we are convinced God created us to manage, then we can more confidently say "No, thank you" to the many other tempting requests.

Sometimes we give ourselves a false sense of guilt for not saying *yes* to requests for our time or expertise, but we are not guilty, any more than we are wrong for saying *no* to the third bag of Doritos in the grocery store. It is hard to set those boundaries at first. Making the budget and sticking to it seems strenuous for a while. But when the budget becomes a *habit,* when we have begun reaping the benefits of living within our means, we will soon see that *no* as the most important part of our freedom. It is the key to the resources we need to intentionally live the life God created us for.

No matter what season of life we are in, no matter how varied our obligations, no matter the obstacles we face, God gives us the power to live gloriously within the means He provided us. Our limited time on this earth is a blessing — a precious stewardship of God's image on our lives, every day and every hour.

What does the Bible say?

Read Isaiah 40, Psalm 90, and 1 Corinthians 12.

What does it mean to you?

Journal your answers and discuss with a friend.

1. How does the concept of God's numbering your days make you feel? Are you filled with dread or with hope? Why?
2. Compare how you feel at the end of each day to how you feel when you wake each morning. Are you drained? Excited? Exhausted?
3. Do you look forward to each new day or season, or do you dread it? Why?
4. How often do you take account of your time budget? When are you planning to review your expenditures?
5. Are you in time debt, or do you enjoy a surplus? How well are you managing your resources?
6. List all of your most important relationships. How are you intentionally investing yourself in each one individually?
7. List all of your regular obligations. Are you managing each one well? Are there debts you need to get rid of?
8. Are you achieving your goals and dreams? What changes should you make so you can begin saving for those opportunities?

It is our God-given responsibility to live out the purpose God created for us.

14

Dare to Dream

Since I was a child, I've been fascinated by self-help books. Books contain knowledge, and knowledge is power, and these books claim the power to radically transform our lives. I cannot resist the temptation to look inside, just to make sure they don't contain the hidden secrets that would change everything for the better. Of course, that's rarely the case. In decades of reading, I have not yet found a book that will actually make one healthy, wealthy, and wise. A few are truly useful, some are helpful, and others are mostly trash. I have not yet, however, found a book from which I could not learn *something,* even if that *something* is *how not to write a book.*

When I browse the library bookshelves each week, I find myself wandering past the cookbooks and exercise manuals, diet volumes and cleaning guides (maybe I should slow down and reconsider these) to peruse again the selection on leadership, influence, and productivity. *How to make your life count* is a weighty topic, a question we wrestle with all day and ponder late into the night. Do I matter? Does what I do make a difference? Can I leave behind a lasting impact?

But those books on that bookshelf aren't written for us. We find ourselves frustrated and disillusioned by the image of upper-middle-aged, upper-middle-class, upper-society men on the back covers, telling us how to make the first six-figure income or million-dollar profit; fit all the board meetings, mergers, and acquisitions into a busy executive schedule; and land the title or political position that will define success. Or we find a few volumes from women, some of whom we recognize from their Facebook picture, and glance past their bio screaming *best-seller* and *TV star* to flip through the pages on how to build a large business and super-social-media following and jewelry line and paper products to illustrate success.

We know that's not *our* success. That's not the life we want. So we turn away from the *make your life count* section of the library or bookstore and walk with sagging shoulders to the periodical section to choose a pretty magazine with which to divert ourselves while we latte-drink away our discouragement.

I have followed this exact pattern every week at the library and every month at the bookstore for the past eight years. Religiously. I have the coffee addiction and stacks of magazines to prove it. I felt this growing dissatisfaction, then restlessness, then outrage. It began spilling into date night with my husband and coffee chats with my friends. *Where are the books for us? Where is the leadership/influence/productivity manual for honest, hard-working, sincere Christian women who know their lives count but they just want help and encouragement?*

Where is truth in the midst of all the world's lies and pressure and empty promises?

I Know You Are Out There

I know there are many of us who love the Lord, lust after our husbands, adore our children, cling to our friends, pray fervently, study hard, and work our tails off to see our lives, our homes, our families, and our ministries make a difference.

We are doing the work, *we are making the difference,* but sometimes we are afraid to say it out loud. It doesn't seem . . . seemly. It feels prideful to exalt the humble work of homemaking and ministry. It goes against our biblical principles to promote Christian influence publicly.

But as our daughters grow older and our friends around us falter in discouragement, this heart cry takes an even more urgent tone. If we hesitate to stand up and give voice to our purpose, our calling, our creative mandate for ourselves, *we dare not be silent for the next generation.* We cannot leave our daughters, our friends, and our sisters in Christ with this false choice between denying their God-given talents and abilities *or* following the world's crowded path to self-exaltation.

It is our God-given responsibility to live out the purpose God created for us. We simply must catch God's vision for our lives, each one of us, then work daily to make that a reality.

Envision. My friend Jessie virtually slaps me through the Facebook messenger every time I use that word. She's sick and tired of being told to *envision* her life, when all she can see is the laundry and Legos, stacking bills and sticky boys that fill her days. She can't even *envision* a full night's sleep when she closes her eyes.

Those self-help books we pass up at the booksellers are full of envisioning exercises. We're told to envision the perfect day and write it down, then start living it step-by-step until our dreams become reality. But every mom knows that doesn't even work for five minutes, because before coffee even finishes brewing each morning one of our family members or appliances has already thrown a wrench in the plans. The chances of living out one perfect day are less than the chances of our winning the lottery — without purchasing a ticket.

We will never live a perfect day, but that doesn't mean we won't live the perfect life God plans for us. *Perfect* must be radically redefined just like *success* and *happy* and *beauty* and *time* and all the other measurements of our life. What if the relationships and work and family and home and ministry and neighbors we have right now are God's perfect plan for our life? What if our painful circumstances and people and past all accentuate His glorious image within us? And what if our perfect day is reflecting God's person in the midst of it all? What if this isn't chaos, but rather a beautifully orchestrated, intricately timed performance of God's order and beauty?

Can we envision that?

When we were younger, we dared to dream. We gave ourselves and our childhood friends extravagant permission to wildly, boldly declare the impossible *possible.* But as we grew, we increasingly encountered roadblocks to our dreams. We learned how hard life is, how rare the chances, how expensive the cost. One by one, we laid aside our dreams.

Then we laid aside dreaming altogether.

Keep on Dreaming!

But it was always God's plan for us to dream. When we dream, we practice our original purpose — being God's image on earth. Because God dreams, and He plans, as He did imagine all of creation and mankind and His chosen ones and the redemptive plan and our eternal lives with Him. We dream because we are like God.

And God's children have always dared to dream extravagantly. Jacob dreamed of heavenly ones ascending and descending the ladder, then later he wrestled one for himself. Joseph dreamed of leading his family, and one day dared provide for an entire nation. Esther imagined she might win a beauty pageant, and perhaps convince the greatest emperor of her time to spare a minority group from annihilation. Isaiah dreamed of worship before the throne of God, Peter dreamed of the Gentiles joining God's people, and John dreamed of Christ's glorious reign on earth.

We may not dream of ruling the country or ascending into heaven, but we should dream. If we are sensitive to the leading of the Spirit, if we earnestly seek God's will for our lives, if we wrestle with the incongruities of truth and failure around us, we cannot help but dream of a better reality. We dream of change in our marriage. We dream of unity in our church. We dream of rebuilding neighborhoods, feeding the homeless, and adopting the orphans. We dream of the lives our children will lead; we imagine the grandparents we will become.

After eight years of frustration at the bookstores, I began to dream of a book, the book I really wanted to read — a book to share with my friends, to pass on to my daughter. I began talking with my husband and my friends about the book. I dared hope that one day I might even write it myself.

The dream scared me. The more I examined it, the more I doubted it. Writing is hard, but publishing is harder. As I continued praying about the vision, I summoned the courage to whisper my dream to others. I found many women who shared the same vision, and over one dozen friends began praying regularly for the dream to become a reality.

Now I couldn't deny the dream, because it was no longer my own. If I dared dismiss it now, these faithful prayer warriors would, justifiably, rebuke me for quitting God's work. I was painfully accountable for fulfilling my responsibility to the dream.

So my word of advice is this: If you want to deny God's purpose for your life, if you are ready to quit the work God gave you to do, be sure you don't tell your dream to anyone who prays.

On the other hand, if you want to see God work mightily on your behalf, answering your heart's desire above and beyond what you ask or think, seek His face, know His will, and commit with others in prayer for the undertaking. These prayers and messages of encouragement remind me every day that *our dreams are not our own.* God's will for our lives is not *our plan.* For how many of us would look around ourselves mid-afternoon and say, "Yep, this is exactly the way I expected my life to be." No, indeed, our dreams stem from God's plan and God molds them and us into His image for our lives.

What dreams do we dismiss? The ideas for an inspirational song, the burden for a Sunday school class topic, the tug to adopt a child, the hope for a ministry-oriented retirement age. Do we brush away the business concept, ministry plan, or family project because it appears too daunting? Have we lost the ability to dream?

Many years ago, I found myself in that position. Painful people, circumstances, and trials had beaten me down. Discouragement and disillusionment had left me disenchanted. I no longer wanted to dream because I feared the disappointment of loss. My husband began regularly casting small visions before me — small, meaningful ways I could make a difference and see a difference. *You can make friends with this neighbor. You can teach this child his multiplication facts. You could send an article to this one publication. You can play your violin in this church.* Even when the simple steps of life seemed insurmountable, I forced myself to try his dream out and see if it was possible. And it was.

One dream-come-true led to another. Gradually, I regained my ability to envision God's working in me and through me. I claimed hope for a life of meaning and significance within His plan. Each dream realized built greater faith, as I knew experientially that God has a perfect plan for my imperfect life.

We all come to dreamless places, times in our life when the obstacles and difficulties around us make envisioning even a good night's sleep or pain-free day impossible. This trial, too, is common to man. Moses traded his ambitions for a wilderness 40 years wide before God cast a new vision for his life. Ruth exchanged her ideals of raising an affluent family for becoming a migrant worker until her mother-in-law hatched a better plan. Peter, James, and John, disillusioned by Christ's death, turned back to their mundane fishing jobs. We cannot always see around the obstacles looming over us, and the clouds of the Curse often cast shadows over God's intended purpose.

How do we regain the dream? How can we envision God's purpose for us in the midst of laundry, leftovers, bills, illness, and tragedy?

First of all, we must reclaim our primary relationship. We cannot capture God's vision for us if we cannot find Him in our lives. When we are faced with discouragement and disillusionment, when our dreams are shattered and we've lost our way, that is when we must flee to Christ.

Balancing It All

In those wilderness times, make devotional reading and Bible study a priority. Find a Bible reading plan or devotional and work through it faithfully until God's voice comes through clearly. Intentionally memorize verses and meditate on God's truth to combat the lies around you.

In addition to Bible reading, practice the habit of prayer. Set aside multiple times a day to pray, and make this an intentional part of your schedule. Keep lists of requests for others as well as for yourself. And when your words run dry from the parched desert of your soul, open Psalms and pray each one aloud. Retrain your heart to cry aloud to God throughout the day, casting each burden and fear repeatedly before Him until the song of praise rises again from your soul.

While refreshing your spiritual life, be sure to nurture your physical body, as well. Balance healthy diet, ample sleep, and regular exercise. As God's image, your triune body, soul, and spirit need unified support to regain their full capacity.

Then, while you begin recovering your relationship with God and your physical health, nurture your most critical relationships. Share your struggle with your spouse, talk about your fears and disappointments with your closest friend, seek advice from godly counselors. Listen carefully for common themes, suggestions that repeatedly come up. Those outside your journey can see how far you have come and may even catch a glimpse of where God is taking you.

Finally, while you are waiting for a fresh vision of God's purpose for your life, take advantage of the opportunities He gives you today — the class that needs a substitute teacher, the shut-in that needs a visit, the mother that needs babysitting help, the ministry right before you that needs a hand. As long as your vision for God's plan is clouded, you don't know what each small act may lead toward. So in faith, take the tasks God brings before you for His glory, and wait for His direction for more.

Waiting in the wilderness takes time. Every step in my book dream took weeks or even months of waiting in prayer. I waited in limbo for years before ascertaining if God wanted me to play my violin again. Moses aged 40 years in his wilderness, and Joseph literally grew up in slavery. Sometimes, the path is cleared quickly, like when Jesus sought out Peter on his boat and told him to quit fishing and start feeding His people. But usually God changes us and prepares us for the dream through the school of waiting.

The waiting and praying and resting and reflecting changes us, and the trials that drove us to the wilderness change us. When we allow God to refine us through our tribulations, when we pray for Christlikeness in our pain, we see Him prepare us through those troubles. Our misshapen homes and painful relationships and imperfect lives point us in a new direction — a different path God intends for us to follow.

This is what James reminds us in his first chapter. Our testing periods produce endurance, perseverance, patience, and faith that God is working all to His purpose. We know He is for us, that He works mightily on our behalf, because we have seen His faithfulness in preserving us during these times.

We learn humility in our reliance on God through the wilderness. Like Paul said, our sickness and rejection and poverty and discouragement drive us to our knees; our weakness reveals God's strength (2 Corinthians 12:10).

The painful trials we face, as we yield to the Spirit's working through them, produce Christ-likeness in our hearts and lives. I am more sensitive to my relationship with my children because of what I learned from my mother. I am compassionate toward those who serve with me in ministry because of the lessons I learned from a bully. There are some lessons in life we can only learn through experience, and these experiences point us toward the purpose of God's glory.

The lessons of pain and the school of waiting last longer than we wish, but at the end God grants us His vision, a new dream for a life of impact. We are His creation, intentionally placed in this time and space to reveal Him, to reflect His glory all around, to enjoy Him now and for eternity. That is a purpose greater than any hardback in the bookstore, more powerful than any five-step plan, more sure than any investment money can buy.

God dreamed us before the world began, and He casts a vision before us of the impact we make for Him. That is reality. That is our life. That's how we rock ordinary every day and become extraordinary in His hands.

What does the Bible say?

Read John 14–17.

What does it mean to you?

Journal your answers and discuss with a friend.

1. How does *dreaming* or *envisioning your future* make you feel right now? Fearful? Discouraged? Excited? Why?

2. Do you have a vision for how God is using you right now? Write down what God is doing through you in these areas, the ways you are making a difference in the lives of others:
    a. Your marriage
    b. Your children
    c. Your extended family
    d. Your friends
    e. Your church
    f. Your community
    g. Your work
3. In chapter 1, how did you define *success*? How do you define *the perfect life*? Has that changed or grown through your study in this book? More importantly, does your definition line up with God's reality for you?
4. If you have stopped dreaming, why? What is standing in the way of seeing God's plan for your life right now?
5. If you are in the wilderness of waiting, get busy! You have some rebuilding to do!
    a. What is your Bible reading plan?
    b. What times during the day will you pray? What prayer aids will you use?
    c. How will you monitor your diet?
    d. What exercise plan are you following?
    e. Who are you confiding in? List the safe people in your life who will speak God's truth into your soul.
    f. What opportunities has God placed in your path right now?
6. What dream scares you? Who is praying over it with you?
7. Look around you — who needs a fresh dream? Which of your family members or friends is struggling through their wilderness? Who is fearful of the vision God gave them? How can you support their growth in Christ?

A Note of Special Thanks

Or, The extraordinary birth of one ordinary book

This isn't my book. It's your book, the tale of how extraordinary your life is every ordinary day. Like I told you in the last chapter, this book was a long time coming. God used so many people to bring this together and to speed this book into your hands.

First of all, God had to teach me these things. And most of those lessons came from my husband, David. You've seen me talk about how awesome he is throughout the chapters, but I can't do him justice. Every time I imagine God's amazing grace, I picture David, and I weep for joy at happily ever after. Thank you for teaching me love, honey. And then there's the children. . . . Thank you for putting up with my "writing time," Gian, Adana, Leandro, and Xzavian, and for reminding me when it was time for supper. You already know that you guys rock.

I have so many praying friends who love me through my failings and who show me real life faith every day. Angela and Faith, your prayers and encouragement lift me up and keep me going. Joanna, for holding me steady in the middle of the craft fair when I literally shook with fear over this prospect, thank you for reminding me then and often since that *our book is already written.* Sarah, you are my forever bosom friend. If you don't sell this to Rollings Reliable Baking Company, I won't tattoo "Rocking Ordinary" on your baby.

Israel Wayne, I can't thank you enough for introducing me to New Leaf Press. I am in awe of the work they do, putting "Ink on Paper to Touch Eternity." I'm forever grateful to Tim Dudley for taking a chance with such an ordinary mom writer, and to Laura Welch and Craig Froman for cleaning me up and making me look respectable for company. But most of all, I'm super in debt to Randy Pratt and Jennifer White for casting a vision before me of how God will empower women through this message.

Writing is hard, but becoming an author is harder. Mary DeMuth, thank you for mentoring me, guiding me, teaching me, and praying for me through the hard words and messy manuscripts. I'm a better writer for knowing you, but I'm a braver woman for praying with you. Thank you seems so small. I owe you a lot of Chipotle.

The most extraordinary launch team ever assembled is known as ROLT, but I call them all my bestest friends. Alanna, Amanda, Amy D, Amy W, Anne, Ashley, Audrey, Ayla, Bethany, Betsy, Betty D, Betty E, Brenda, Bridgette, Catherine, Cece, Chloe, Cindy, Courtney, Dana, Dawn, Debbie, Deb, Deena, Diana, Donna, Elizabeth, Emilie, Emily, Eva, Flora, Glenda, Heather H, Heather P, Holly C, Holly D, Jackie, Jana, Jennie W, the other Jennie W, Jennifer C, Jennifer S, Jenny V, Jeri M, Jordan, Karla, Kassi, Katrina L, Katrina M, Kendra, Kerry, Khadijah, Kimberly, KT, LaKisha, Laura, Laurie, Lia, Linda F, Linda U, Lindsay, Lynley, Marie, Maritza, McKenzie, Melanie, Melissa K, Melissa W, Misti, Pam, Patricia, Patti, Pattie, Patty, Rebecca, Redonna Rhonda, Sally, Starla, Stephanie, Theresa, Tifffany Tina, Tori, Traci, Tracy, Trisha, Victoria, and Yvie. Wow — how amazing it is that God brought us together! You all rock. Especially Jenny Herman, who made happy sense of the chaos our parties easily dissolved into. We must stay in close touch.

And now you have it. May God's grace and unconditional love be near to you today and every ordinary day to come.

Love,
Lea Ann
leaann@lagarfias.com

Lea Ann Garfias is a homeschool graduate and homeschool mom who is still learning how to adult. As a long-time ministry leader and writer, she encourages her friends to recognize their lasting impact on the world around them. A writer on homeschooling and Christian family life for over a decade, Lea Ann serves as Features Editor of *Home School Enrichment Magazine*. She lives with her husband David and their four children in the Dallas area, where she serves as principal violinist in her local symphony and as church choir director. Lea Ann enjoys connecting with like-minded women through speaking engagements and through her website lagarfias.com.

OPEN & GROW

Rocking Ordinary Small Group Kit
978-0-89221-749-6 **$49.99**

Leaders Guide
978-0-89221-748-9 **$11.99**

DVD (120 min.)
713438-10234-4 **$25.99**

Rocking Ordinary Book
978-0-89221-744-1 **$12.99**

Includes: Leader's guide, *Rocking Ordinary: Holding It Together With Extraordinary Grace* book, and DVD of author Lea Ann Garfias. This study is designed to be done in either 4 or 8 parts depending on how the leader wants to work through the study. Ordinary is extraordinary is the message of this study and is designed to encourage women that they have significant influence in their ordinary, everyday lives.

New Leaf Press
A Division of New Leaf Publishing Group
www.newleafpress.net